Do NOTHING… To Get EVERYTHING!

You've been Suckered By Your Own Thoughts… Here's How to Stop It!

Amir Karkouti

What Others Say About Doing NOTHING:

If you know that fundamentally there is nothing to seek, you have settled your affairs.
~Zen Saying

Sitting peacefully doing nothing, Spring comes and the grass grows all by itself.
~Taoist Saying

All know the way; few actually walk it.
~Just a Saying

Dedicated to...

The person who figures out that this is all a game. The person who figures out that you are the game.

Make the rules, break the rules, when you are the game...you can even have no rules.

Introduction: Part 1

Do not study this book like a textbook. Read it like you're dancing. Have fun with it. Let it just glide between your eyes. Don't give it too much thought. Our "thoughts" about things are what get us into trouble in the first place.

This book will not give you any answers you are looking for. No book can do that.

I think we all secretly know that books aren't a key to happiness, but we still like to read them. We also know that a job will not give us financial stability, and our relationships cannot give us security. If the opposite were true, all rich people would feel stable, all people who are married would have security, and everyone who has read every book on happiness would be bleeding with happiness...

So, why read a book on inner peace if it's not going to make you more peaceful? The same reason you go to see a good movie. You know that it's just a movie — the actors are just acting — but it's still nice to grab popcorn, grab a seat, and enter that world.

The only thing I ask you not to do is punish yourself for years if one of the actors dies in the movie and you become scarred for life.

Hey, wake up! They are just acting; they really didn't die! If you cried to your friends and neighbors about Arnold Schwarzenegger's death in Terminator 1, that would make you look silly. It would also look silly if you found inner peace from a book. This book is just a movie. It's made for fun, for you to maybe enjoy the ride and get a glimpse of what may or may not be.

Don't merely read the words; the secrets aren't going to be hidden there. Read *above* the words, like a song or a painting.

Your curiosity is already kicking in. I can feel it. As I write this, I am curious about what I am going to say right now. Guess what? We are both on the same page. As you read this, you don't know what you are going to read next. That's the beauty of discovery. Thank you for letting me jump onboard with you.

I hope we meet again together. Maybe we'll meet somewhere in thought. Actually, the only way we see the world is in thought. Think about that for a moment...

Amir Karkouti

"The quieter you become, the more you can hear."

~Ram Dass

"Just remain here, and you will be surprised. If you are just now here, all thoughts disappear, because all thoughts are either of the past or of the future. No thought is of the present."

~ Osho

"But the attitude of faith is to let go, and become open to truth, whatever it might turn out to be!"

~Alan Watts

WELCOME
Introduction: Part 2

This is not your ordinary book. This is your life. It has no real ending or beginning. I want you to start it where you want. As you probably already figured out...there are no chapters, and there is no right way to read this.

But there is something you might get from this book. It might not even be when you are reading it. You'll have a thought, you might get pissed off, or get a warm feeling. You might not get anything at all. But don't be surprised if you start to see the world a different way. Maybe you can give this book the credit...but I wouldn't so quickly.

Like a good bowl of soup, the soup is only as good as the person who prepared it and stirred it and looked over it. This will be your job. I'll just supply some of the ingredients. You're going to have to do most of the cooking!

The magic will not be in the words. I promise you that. If you try to "get it," there is nothing to get. I hope as you continue to read this you'll understand.

If you need some help or you are a "metaphor learner," then I would say that this book will get as close to how to find true, innate understanding as you'll ever find. Obviously, words will never be the totality of understanding. It's like someone trying to tell you what hunger feels like. I'm sure some authors can do a pretty damn good job, but nothing explains hunger like the actual experience. That goes for thirst, digestion, love, hurt, UNDERSTANDING, and everything in between.

This is not just an ordinary book, and you are not just an ordinary person. If you think you're ordinary, then you just haven't figured out how amazing you are. I'm not here to convince you that you are. No amount of words can do that.

But if you let yourself get the insight, you just might agree with me. Than we can laugh about all the dumb shit we've been trying to figure out all of our lives, and live!

Amir Karkouti

The Most Important Chapter in This Book...If There Were Chapters in the Book

Moment to Moment
You Are Either in Life or in Thought...
One Brings You Joy, the Other Brings Misery

When I was 20 years old, I finally decided to get laser eye surgery. Gone were the days of finding cool glasses, or picking between hard or soft contacts.

To my surprise, the surgery lasted less than 10 minutes. Soon I was going to have perfect vision, but not until my eyes were fully healed.

When the surgery was complete, my doctor gave me a pair of glasses that made the room almost pitch black. I could see just enough to make out shapes and not bump into things. Besides that, everything else looked pretty hazy.

It was interesting to go around in these glasses. My world was exactly same. I would still talk to my friends on the phone, go to the same restaurants, and walk clumsily around my kitchen, but with a different reality — a reality that was dark and fuzzy.

The reason I knew not to get depressed or worry about this new reality was I knew that eventually I was going to be able to take the glasses off and see more of my reality again; a clearer one, one that allowed me to see more of the world in perfect color.

People who are depressed, experience PTSD or anxiety, are living in a world that isn't allowing them to see it the way I see the world. I want to make it clear that it's not because they want to or choose to.

When we experience a traumatic event, we rely on our thinking to get us out of it. The thinking, the voices, and the thoughts in our heads are what perpetuate the grim reality we so eagerly want to escape.

We end up breaking down and getting help. The therapist or doctor tells us that we are depressed and we need to think better thoughts or not think at all. The problem is, our brains are hardwired to think. To try to remove thinking would require more thinking. This creates a perpetual whirlwind for many who are troubled with illnesses. What normally occurs is they believe it is incurable... which creates more thinking.

We all have chatter in our heads every single millisecond of our existence. For the most part, these voices are harmless. They may say things like, "That woman (or man) is good-looking," "I want to kill my boss," "I think that puppy is cute," "I don't feel like I can live anymore," etc.

When you start to believe that the voices in your head are more than just voices in your head, that's when the trouble begins.

The reality for many suicidal people is that the voices in their head tell them to kill themselves, so they start to believe it. I have had moments where my voices in my head said the same thing, and thank God I knew they were just voices in my head. I remember when I was young and my mom said to me, "If someone told you to jump off a bridge, would you do it?" My answer was always no. So, why would the answer be any different when that "someone" is the voice in my head?

When the voices or thoughts that are just floating around in your brain are not given any power, your everyday life has color and clarity. Sanity and well-being become the natural side-effect of life.

As soon as you believe that one particular thought out of the 70,000 you will have today means more than any other, you have just put on the dark, grim glasses my eye doctor gave me that changed the outlook of my reality.

For many people, the reason that positive psychology, exercise, walking away (or whatever ritual you decide to do) only works for the moment is because you are still in the same paradigm of believing that your voices or thoughts will bring you resolution. The problem with trying to do the above solutions is that they are not solutions at all, because you are still in life with the glasses on. Although it may appear that you have changed your environment, you'll eventually realize that the glasses are still on your face, which will take you back to the same place you were before.

The solution is so paradoxical that we often miss it. The solution is so close to us, we ignore it. The solution is so simple that even the most complicated and decorated psychologists have dismissed it.

Our grief, depression, and anxiety can only live in one place. The illnesses we believe we have are just thoughts floating in our heads. The only way they can be activated and come alive is if you believe you need to engage in that thought. Don't get me wrong — the world can seem very hard and painful. If you drop a rock on your foot, you can be a victim and say the rock did this to you and believe it. The rock is only a rock, but the thought you create, listen to, and believe gives you the feeding mechanism to make the rock more than it is.

Even though events in life may seem more important than a rock, please keep in mind that, as bad as the outside world may appear, it can only have the meaning it can have with the collaboration of your thoughts, your engagement in those thoughts, and the constant reminder that the thoughts you decided to make real are actually real.

But the world you see is what it is. The smell and color of the feeling can only be created via thought. This may be hard to hear, and you may want to dismiss it, like I did. But when you see that the glasses you have on don't need to be on you anymore, or have that little insight that lets you know it's just the glasses on your head (or the thoughts inside your head) that are making the world look a certain way, you may wake up and say to yourself, *I don't need them anymore. They are no longer useful to me.*

You have the power to remove the glasses of thought blurring your vision by not giving that particular thought more power than the next one.

Many questions arise from this understanding.

"So, do I try to forget my thoughts? How do I accomplish that?"

There is no need to forget your thoughts. The reality is when you are trying to forget your thoughts, you are keeping them alive.

There is nothing to do but acknowledge the thought. I want you to understand that I have thoughts similar to your thoughts. The only difference is, I know it's just my brain doing brain things and nothing else, whereas you may have given the same process more meaning. In other words, if I see a car accident and five months later I think about it, then start to have thoughts that my mother may be in a car accident, and I call her and I can't get a hold of her, my thinking tells me she is really in pain. I'll call my dad and if he doesn't pick up either, I'll go into a whirlwind of more thinking and listen to the thoughts that tell me he was also in the car. You can clearly see that I made the whole scenario up in my head and started to believe it. For many, if they continue in this thought pattern, it will turn into a panic attack, which creates more thoughts and noise, and so on.

If my mom calls in an hour and says her phone was turned off because she was at a movie...go back and read how silly the above paragraph sounds now. Most of our reality when we are in pain and misery is not when we are living in *life*, but when we are living in *thought*. Our pain is created moment-to-moment in real time. Your past that you relive can only come back alive in the thinking you are having right now. The moods you feel — both high and low — create the decisions you make in that moment. That's why when you are in a good mood, the decisions look a lot different than when you are in a low mood. In other words, the outside world doesn't have much bearing on your decisions as much as the state of your mood level when you decided to make a decision. The state is dictated by how much you decide to feed that particular thought you are having at the moment. If you don't feed into a thought, then by design, the whirlwind cannot start. The solution is so simple we often miss it.

There is nothing more to do than to hear the voice in your head and say, "I'm too busy to listen to you right now because I need to know what's going on in my life. If you don't have something nice to say to me right now, I don't have time to hear it. Try calling back later."

It's that simple.

I will be dumbfounded if you can bring me any person who has PTSD, stress, anxiety, or depression who uses another way to get themselves back to that state of illness. I'll also be dumbfounded to know that there is another mechanism to get them out of that state other than when they are not in that thought.

If you have watched CNN, you'll notice the news on the main part of the screen and the ticker tape below showing sentences rapidly moving along. If you can imagine the main screen is your life, and the ticker tape your thoughts, you'll notice that the more you pay attention to the main screen, the less important the ticker becomes. The opposite is true, as well. The more you notice the ticker, the less you see the big screen. Many believe that you need to stop the ticker or remove the ticker in order to feel good. The reality is, the ticker (our thoughts) is playing every second that we are conscious. It's the way the system was created. To try to remove the ticker is not a choice. Realizing the ticker or our weightless, immaterial thoughts may feel real, but don't have much power — this creates a space where more of our life is enjoyed. At any given moment, if you decide to engage in your thoughts, your well-being will either be positive or negative. Your feelings, therefore, have nothing to do with the outside world, but are "colored" depending on the engagement of any particular thought that is coming through your mind. The trick becomes realizing that when you don't engage in that thought in the moment, new thinking will come up automatically. There is nothing to be done by you. This explains why sometimes traffic seems upsetting at times depending on the thought you are engaging in, and at other times seems like no big deal. It has nothing to do with traffic; it has everything to do with the thought you are occupied with at that moment. Think back at any situation that seems so terrible at the time and you will be able to trace it back to the thinking you were in at that instant.

Moment to moment, we are either in life or in thought. One will bring you joy, the other will bring misery.

I don't want you to believe me — no, not at all. I want you to trust in yourself. I want you to humor yourself and don't be afraid of the voices.

The voices are the soundtrack of your thinking,

nothing more.

Some days they are loud, other days you can barely hear them. When they seem loud and they are screaming at you and you don't like the music, just listen like a third party. You don't need to engage in the fight. My friends put on music in their car I don't enjoy, but it would seem silly to think their music is harmful. Listen to the voices. It's okay to listen. Hear what they have to say.

If the voices say you're worthless, you're scared, you are seeing things, the world hates you, you should kill yourself; you always have the choice to decide whether to believe them or not.

You have a choice whether or not to believe the voices in your head.

You have a choice to decide whether the guy inside is being mean and it's worth your time to engage.

If your thoughts sound like a bully or a telemarketer, let him know you don't have time for that right now.

You don't need to believe the words that are coming out of his mouth. The thoughts don't really have a mouth to begin with. As real as it sounds, it's not real.

But the choice to engage in the illusion is very real.

As soon as you believe that the immaterial thoughts that are arising in your mind can harm you, they affect your physical world. That's when panic arises. That's when depression kicks in. That's when you feel the effects of PTSD.

If this paradigm I propose is true, the idea to have a client relive a past after going through a traumatic event would not make sense. The idea that they need to bring up a past that no longer exists — that can ONLY exist via thought in the present moment — is only a recipe for disaster. People who get bouts of depression feel most depressed in the depressed thought in that moment. People who feel the pain of their PTSD feel it in the moment in which they are having their episodes, in thought. People who get panic attacks only get them when they engage in that thought at the moment. That's why when all the people above are not in that particular thought anymore, the episodes go away. So, where is the sense to have anyone relive a traumatic situation as a way to reduce that particular thought?

As soon as the understanding arises that they are just voices with no real harm, like waking up from a terrible dream...

...you'll find something really funny happens. The voice will try to bring more hurtful words to you, because it wants to engage. Like a person who doesn't shut up when you are talking to them, just let the voice know, "Hey, thanks for talking, but I'm kinda busy right now dealing with something in the outside world. I can't do both right now because you're making me lose my concentration. I might come back and play later or when you have nice things to say."

I am going to give you an example from a client I just met with a bit ago. Don't dismiss this story because it seems silly.

*Imagine This:

A client comes to me to resolve this issue about his anxiety. Before we begin our session, he wants to let me know about this dream he had about his girlfriend. He tells me that he is in a coffee shop and his girlfriend gets approached by both Saddam Hussein and Justin Bieber. Both of them want to have sex with his girlfriend in the dream. He goes on to tell me that he was concerned about what he should do. If he didn't allow Saddam to have sex with his girlfriend, he was afraid he would be killed. On the other hand, he didn't want Justin Bieber to have sex with her because he would have to tell his friends. As he continued, the last thing he said was, "So, what should I have done?" What if he is totally serious? I'd look at him and say, "Is there really anything to do? It's a dream and it's not real. To find a resolution for this imaginary problem is a waste of both of our time." What if he agreed and proceeded to tell me about his anxiety. What if he told me that he has negative thoughts throughout the day and that he doesn't know what to do with them? For me to find a solution about what he needs to do with his thoughts is the same type of solution he was looking for when he had the dream. It's just a thought. What do you want me to do about it? As soon as you realize it's just a thought and you let it go, you will allow the possibility of new thought to arise. There is absolutely nothing left to do! The problem with many alternatives in mental health fields is they are too busy engaging in the dream and finding ways to figure out why someone is having those particular thoughts and how to remove them. I would never sit with my client and worry about why he is having a particular dream, because I know that's not where the solution lies. I wouldn't worry about the particular thoughts, because I know the solution doesn't lie there, either.

It would be silly to wake up from a dream and worry about it the rest of the day. The dream has passed, and as soon as you become aware it's a dream, there is nothing else to do. To try to find tools to combat the events in the dream becomes a moot point. Once you realize you were dreaming, that is all that is needed. Once you realize your thoughts are "thoughting" there is no need to combat them or find strength to remove them. Experts are having clients find ways to slay the dragons in their dreams, or gain resilience or willpower to overcome this feeling. As real as the dragons felt in the dream, once you get the understanding that it wasn't real, your efforts to find tools, willpower, or anything, become irrelevant. The only thing needed is the understanding that your brain is having voices going through and one is no more important than any other. Once you gain that understanding, you'll soon realize that the dragon problem was created by you and the solution to slay the dragon is also created by you. In essence, you have created the imaginary hurdle and the imaginary solution to jump the hurdle you put up in the first place, via thought.

This little understanding may save someone's life. This little insight may get rid of years of anger, frustration, and confusion for many (after all, you're only engaging the hurtful thinking, nothing more). This little bit of wisdom allows me to live my life and not live in my thoughts, and it has also done the same for many of my clients.

Please share this understanding with someone who might need it. Please let them know that they are perfectly healthy and that they are not sick. Please let them know that even if people have told them they are crazy, ill, or broken, it's not true. They are as perfect as they can be. There is absolutely nothing wrong with them. They are just walking around with shades on and they don't know it. They are looking for answers when the answers are within their understanding. As soon as a little crack is open in their understanding, the healing process can occur and they will see a whole new world that was impossible to see because they were too busy trying to find the answer in thought — the very same place that was creating the problem.

Moment to Moment you are either in Life or in Thought. One brings Joy, the other Misery. That's just the way the system works.

If you are in the mental health field, please don't dismiss this important paradigm of mental health that is so overly missed. I have been able to help many people (who have been told that they are sick) by helping them get along with their thoughts and not believing everything they hear (even the voices in their heads). People are not sick, they are poisoning themselves with thought and they don't even know they are doing it. Let them know this understanding so they can stop drinking the poison. Instead of looking at people from a mental illness perspective, it's time to see ourselves from a mental *wellness* perspective. We are all healthy. Some of us have engaged in our unhealthy thoughts and others have realized that the thoughts in our heads can't do us harm unless we let them. The solution is not in the tools to combat this illusion, it's in the understanding of seeing the problem for what it is; just a thought...

*Thank you Michael Neill for the inspiration for the dream story.

"YOU DON'T SEE THE WORLD...YOU THINK THE WORLD YOU SEE."

(You can't have it any other way...think about it.)

POOR IGNAZ

Ignaz Semmelweis was a Hungarian physician who figured it all out. The problem was, all the other physicians didn't think so.

Dr. Semmelweis, when working in Vienna General Hospital's first obstetrical clinic, discovered that washing your hands with chlorinated lime solutions, which we now call soap, decreased infant mortality rates by 10%-35%. You see, back then doctors and the established scientific community just didn't believe that soap had any real effects to mortality rates in babies when they were born. Matter of fact, some doctors even got offended at the suggestion that they should wash their hands. After all, doctors have hands that don't need any washing. Additionally, the more established the doctor, the less he needed to do anything to his hands before surgery.

Back in the mid 19th century, the scientific community believed that people got sick from smells, not germs, which at the time nobody knew about. It made sense. After all, people stink when they die and normally smelly dead people mean there are going to be more smelly dead people around. So, doctors and people alike thought that putting flowers and perfume around themselves would get rid of sickness. But Ignaz knew better and nobody would listen.

Now here comes poor Ignaz Semmelweis, with no medical or scientific proof telling them that they had it wrong. He was trying to convince the scientific community that there are little germy thingys on people's hands and that if they used soap, it would remove these little germy guys, which in turn would help infants survive.

But poor Ignaz would not give up. He went from doctor to doctor to tell them that this lime solution (soap) could really help infants. I mean, really help them live! The more he went around telling them, the more the doctors thought he was crazy! Ha-ha, little creatures on people's hands that can get people sick...he sure was crazy!

Well, telling enough people something that might be right when nobody is ready to listen can mean big trouble!

In 1865, poor Ignaz was committed to an insane asylum.

Poor Ignaz ironically died of septicemia at age 47. Septicemia, we now know, could have been avoided if the doctors had just washed their hands with soap.

The moral of the story...read this book and don't laugh too soon. You might be creating your own mental grave because you've held so tightly to established beliefs. Sure, the ideas in this book will sound crazy. They might even sound laughable. I used to be among the people who laughed at poor Ignaz because my thinking paradigm was too small to see the possibilities. Thank goodness I got out of my trap and thank goodness that Louis Pasteur confirmed germ theory and Joseph Lister practiced and operated using hygienic methods with great success. I can't say that I'm as smart as Pasteur or Lister, but I can say that my change in thinking has worked for me — and as soon as others see what I am trying to convey, there is no turning back. I only ask for one favor: keep your mind open and allow for a new paradigm in your own thinking. If you don't like it, you can always go back.

Dr. Ignaz Semmelweis, age 42 in 1860.
Pen sketch by Jenő Dopy.

To know what we do not know is the beginning of wisdom…

RAIN DANCE

One night I decided to plop down on the couch and browse through Netflix. I found a video called *Pururumba*. If you haven't seen it, I highly recommend you check it out. *Pururumba* is about a tribe in the rainforest that nobody has ever seen. That's right, not even the other tribes in the rainforest would dare to cross this imaginary border to see who they were.

A white guy and his cameraman were escorted to this imaginary border, leaving these two men to discover this new territory all on their own.

As you can guess, it got really crazy! First, the tribal leader sees the two guys and he has no idea what to do...their skin is white, which resembles death to them. Second, the tribal leader doesn't know what to do with the guys because the white devils are so nice. Long story short, after a few looks and threats, the tribe is willing to trust the two men and invites them into their world.

Here is the interesting thing: When you look at how basic they live and how superstitious they are, you can see that just a little knowledge could completely transform their view of life, *if* they could just see it. The problem is, they are stuck in their way of thinking. There was one part of the movie where a child was dying from what looked like a simple cold. The problem was the white guys, although they had medicine to help the child, couldn't help. They figured that if the kid still passed after their help, the natives would attribute it to the devil's work. Now here was their bind... if they didn't help and the kid died, the natives would have blamed the white guys anyway, because they showed up right when the kid became ill. They realized that they were damned if they did help, damned if they didn't. So they waited it out to see what happened. Luckily, the kid became better... lucky for them!

Even though they have had no direct association with any other humans ever, they still do the exact same things as all the other humans in many parts of the world. They do rain dances to bring the rain. They chant and light fire to things to remove evil spirits. You know what? Sometimes the rain dances would bless them with rain, and sometimes the smoke removed evil spirits. No animals would come to harm them and nobody would get sick. But of course, when it didn't rain, someone had done the rain dance wrong or the spirits were too strong that day!

When we look at them, we find this silly. For the most part, we don't need to do rain dances in America anymore, because we know that's not how the system works. Regardless how long I dance or sing, rain is going to come or go, based on weather patterns. So you can see how, if you think your actions somehow are connected to the weather, they can also dictate your thinking.

Don't be fooled...the whole story from this movie shows us more about our own rain dances, and how we really haven't progressed much from this kind of thinking. Can you remember a time when you would huff and puff, or scream and pound on your steering wheel when you were stuck in traffic? It's an interesting rain dance, but it won't make the traffic go faster. The system doesn't work that way.

Or, when you read up on books, go to seminars to become a better person...it's a better rain dance than pounding on your steering wheel, but it's still *only* a rain dance. You see, you're trying to get peace of mind from outside yourself; the system just doesn't work that way.

Of course, when your job is stressful and you take it out on your spouse or your kids, and you tell everyone how terrible your life is, and how everyone just has it better, it's justified. Thinking this way will make you feel better (for the moment) by making an environment change, but it's just another rain dance. I see this all the time...everyone does their own personal interpretive dance. Very inspiring! But, again, it's just a rain dance!

If I could give the natives some advice, I would show them how the system works...that with or without the dance, the world is going to weather. The world "weathers" whenever it wants. If the rain dance is something you want to do, by all means do it! Just know that the system doesn't care whether you dance or not, it's going to do what it's going to do. Once you realize that your "thinking" about the outside world doesn't change the outside world and whether you think it's good or bad, you can sit back and stop doing that job. You see, as soon as they realize the weather doesn't work that way, the rain dance seems rather silly. Once you realize that thinking about your outside environment or how the outside world "weathers" with or without your help, you can stop trying to "think" that your dance will change it. Once you get this understanding, something really neat happens. Your body relaxes and gets this innate understanding that you can go around the world essentially enjoying the rain or sunshine. At the end of the day, it's going to do what it's going to do. Once you know that, you can rain dance if you want, but just know that you're doing it because you want to, not for any psychological assistance.

WHAT'S YOUR RAIN DANCE?

"I know you're bored but you better not be doing that rain dance again!"

When Nothing Works!

I'm guessing you've already done everything.

You might have read books, gone to seminars, spoken to friends, co-workers and even your mother...

You have tried vacationing and you've tried taking time off. Even that seems like something to do.

I have a friend who went all the way to Tibet to study with monks to clear his head from all the daily stress. I can completely understand that way of thinking. I've done it and I'm still guilty of doing it.

It makes sense to try to find peace from the outside. After all, there are dozens of ads per second telling you that you should go on your dream vacation and leave where you are to relax. Funny thing about the word "vacation" in the first place. The word starts with the word "vacate," as in to leave the place where you are.

But what if you didn't have to do that? What if where you are is exactly where you need to be to find the ultimate peace?

Now hold on...no need to pull out the patchouli and yoga mat just yet. That's a good way to relax too, but it's not the "real" way to relax.

Are you ready for the secret?

This is what my whole coaching philosophy rests on. This is the foundation of my connection with my clients, to get them where they want to be.

This is the solution to those "aha" moments. This is the solution to that idea you should have come up with two weeks ago.

This is what has you remember the person's name at 3:00 a.m. when you couldn't think of it when you were trying...

Wait, read the last sentence again.

This is what has you remember the person's name at 3:00 a.m. when you couldn't think of it when you were trying...

Most of our inspiration comes when we are doing NOTHING.

Most all of our clear thinking happens when we are not trying. When we have NOTHING on our minds!

We have been suckered into believing we have to try to do something to get an answer...when most answers come when we do nothing.

Don't get me wrong, doing something sometimes works, but look back at the times when you've gotten your best breakthroughs...

It's when you did NOTHING.

Even when you have brainstorming ideas and meetings, you've probably had that feeling when you're driving and you say to yourself...

"SHIT, why didn't I just say that then? Why are all my good answers coming to me now?"

It's probably because you were trying to squeeze brilliance out. It's probably because you were "trying" to relax.

Brilliance, Laughter, Joy, Love, Inspiration, Ideas, "Aha" Moments ... all come from NOTHING!

Now, I don't want you to try to do nothing. Then you are doing something. Nothing happens when nothing happens.

Want to practice? Great!

Listen to a song...
Dance without paying attention to the steps...
Laugh!
Watch kids play!
Fall in love...and notice what is *not* being said to each other.
Go in the shower with the idea of...well... just showering...
Play an instrument or watch someone who is...notice that stream of undoing that goes through their mind.

Kind of strange, I know. We've been taught to do something all of our lives, and that's okay, too.

But try doing NOTHING too!

Once you've discovered doing NOTHING, you'll notice that even when you are doing something, you can enjoy the NOTHINGNESS of it.

In other words, you can do the "dance" of work.

You can be the kid in the playground! Kids are doing something but with nothing on their minds...

Go to work with NOTHING on your mind and do your work. See how things flow. Putting worry on one thought is hopeless. Let the thoughts happen. If you "try" to do something about the thoughts, remind yourself to STOP! Wait for a moment, breathe, and keep going...with nothing on your mind.

I know you've done everything, and you've gotten good at it.

Now try NOTHING...

You'll be surprised how well <u>NOTHING WORKS!</u>

If you think something outside of yourself is the CAUSE of your problem...You will look outside of Yourself for the Answer!

(hint: You Won't Find it there)

EXERCISE #438

THE PROBLEM OF TRYING AND WHY THE SYSTEM DOESN'T WORK THAT WAY...

WHAT YOU NEED TO DO:

YOU NEED TO REMOVE ANY JUDGEMENTS AND JUST TRUST ME AND YOURSELF...YOU CAN DO THIS!

THIS WILL NOT WORK IF YOU DON'T TRY...YOU HAVE TO REALLY BE WILLING TO TRY.

I'M SERIOUS.

OKAY...ARE YOU READY?

WE ARE GOING TO DO AN EXPERIMENT. AFTER THE EXPERIMENT, HOPEFULLY YOU'LL REALIZE HOW SILLY IT IS. THEN YOU WILL APPLY IT TO YOUR LIFE AND REALIZE IT'S THE SAME THING.

THAT'S ALL I'M GOING TO SAY!

HOW TO MAKE THE HAIR ON YOUR HEAD GROW FASTER WITH SOME SIMPLE STEPS...

ALL RIGHT, FOLLOW THESE STEPS:

1) SIT DOWN SOMEWHERE AND GET COMFORTABLE
2) TENSE YOUR WHOLE BODY FROM HEAD TO TOE AND MAKE A TIGHT FIST. I MEAN LIKE A REALLY TIGHT FIST LIKE YOU'RE CRACKING A NUT!

3) I NEED YOU TO REALLY CONCENTRATE AND MAKE YOUR BODY EVEN TIGHTER!
4) NOW I WANT YOU TO TRY TO MAKE THE HAIR ON YOUR HEAD GROW FASTER! IF NOTHING HAPPENS...FOLLOW STEPS 1-3!
5) OKAY, IF THAT DIDN'T WORK, ASK YOURSELF WHY? WE'LL TRY SOMETHING ELSE. GO AHEAD AND RELAX.
6) WHAT I WANT YOU TO DO NOW IS GO BACK TO A RELAXED POSITION AND CLOSE YOUR EYES.
7) NOW PUT A SMILE ON YOUR FACE AND SAY POSITIVE THINGS ABOUT YOURSELF AND HOW EASY AND EFFORTLESSLY YOUR HAIR WILL GROW INSTANTLY. DO THAT NOW!
8) TAKE A FEW MOMENTS TO REALLY USE SOME POSITIVE AFFIRMATIONS TO MAKE YOURSELF GROW YOUR HAIR! COME ON!
9) IS IT WORKING?
10) I KNOW, I THINK YOU NEED TO READ SOME BOOKS ON HOW TO GROW YOUR HAIR, OR MAYBE GO TO A SEMINAR TO FIND OUT THE SECRETS...DON'T YOU THINK THAT WILL DO IT?
11) DO YOU KNOW WHY?

(answer on the next page)

BECAUSE THAT'S NOT HOW THE SYSTEM WORKS!

You find this silly. You know that your hair will grow at the rate it will.

You know it's silly to think that squeezing arbitrarily is not going to grow it any faster!

You know that thinking positive thoughts about your hair might make you feel good, but it will not grow your hair faster.

It's just not the way the system works!

Did you know your thoughts work the same way? That's right!

Oh, here we go...you're ready to battle that one.

You're probably saying to yourself, *It's not the same thing...I can control my thoughts.*

Really? Okay, then if you can control your thoughts...tell your thoughts to stop reading this and making it look like a bunch of nonsense. Keep scrolling through this book and tell yourself that you are no longer going to comprehend the words on this page!

Come on, do it!

You can't!

Your thoughts are going to do what they are going to do. You know that.

Have you ever had a bad day and you think about it, and think about it, and think about it (oh it's bad...you have no idea how bad my day is).

Then...

ALL OF A SUDDEN...

You see a car crash and you look back and say,

"HOLY SHIT, THAT ACCIDENT IS TERRIBLE!"

And you totally forget about your day... until you remind yourself of it and you went right back to worrying about it?

Your mind changed what it wanted to think about and it did...with or without your permission. That's how the system works.

You were trained to think you can do it yourself, but really, your brain thinks and has billions of thoughts per second, with or without your help...just like your hair growing.

Your mind is going to think, and your hair will grow. You can try to pretend that you have control of it. Good luck! You might feel good about trying to control it. You may feel good for a bit by having good thoughts about your day...but just one thought can change everything, and you know it.

So, is this a gloomy thing?

It's better than that!

You see, going back to your hair, how nice is it to know that whether you try to do something or not, your hair is going to grow at the pace it naturally does?

YOU DON'T HAVE TO DO A DAMN THING!

NOTHING!

It will do it all by itself!

No amount of physical squeezing, affirmations or good thoughts will change it.

You can now remove yourself from that job of trying to control the pace of your hair! You can give that up. YOU'RE FREE NOW to do so!

Your thoughts are the same way!

Your thoughts will run all day, and you don't need to do anything about it.

That means you can stand by and just notice your thoughts and not give them much meaning, unless you want to. But at the end of the day, your brain will have millions of them. Trying to control them is like trying to catch water in a net!

This is not a lesson, it's just a fact...it's the way the system works. It's when we try to grasp our thoughts that we get into trouble. Think back to the times when you just had a great time. How did you do it?

That's right!

NO THINKING...JUST DOING happened!

It's a good feeling to know that you don't have to put so much emphasis on one particular thought anymore, because another will come up in merely a millisecond. So, what's the point of worrying about that particular one? It's not going to last that long, unless of course you try to make it last. Even when you try to make it last, you have hundreds of thoughts passing through. The only difference is, you're not noticing them because you've suckered yourself into one thought.

Okay, you've tried to hold on to thoughts to achieve inner peace...

You can now remove yourself from that job of trying to control your thoughts! You can give that up. YOU'RE FREE NOW to do so!

The Truth is Your Wisdom Unveiled, When You Remove All of the Noise

~Michael Neill

What a FIREFIGHTER Can Teach You About Mindfulness

I know when I see an accident on the street the first thing that comes to my mind is curiosity. I'm curious to know if they are okay, how they are, how their family must feel when they get the phone call.

I remember driving by a crash where the firefighters where surrounding the car so bystanders couldn't see the mess.

I tried not to look, but I did anyway. I wish I hadn't. I saw a guy on a motorcycle who was ripped in half, literally, and he was still alive!

I was freaking out in my mind! I have no idea what I would have done if I had been the first person on the scene!

I know that I would have probably have been a mess and thought a million thoughts and would have been shaken up...

I want to ask if the script was flipped around and you were the person on the bike, which firefighter you would want helping you out. The firefighter who is screaming, freaking out, running around in his head, scrambling to get you back in shape? Or the firefighter who knows that screaming, freaking out, running around in his head, and scrambling to get you back in shape will not help the situation?

If you picked the second firefighter, then you are smart — or at least want a better chance at living. You and I both know that when someone has a higher level of thinking, a place where you don't allow yourself to get in the way, you will come up with better answers to situations. You and I both know that by looking at the event for what it is and not adding any clouds to our thinking, we are in a better state to make decisions. You and I both know that the first firefighter would most likely get fired. Nobody needs a person who uses their useless thoughts to make decisions.

With that being said:

WHY DO SO MANY THINK THAT SCREAMING AND FREAKING OUT WILL HELP THE SITUATIONS IN THEIR RELATIONSHIPS?

WHY DO SO MANY THINK THAT SCREAMING AND FREAKING OUT HAS ANY RELEVANCE OR ASSISTANCE TO *ANY* SITUATION?

WHY DO SO MANY PEOPLE THINK THAT SCREAMING AND FREAKING OUT CHANGES THE EVENTS OUTSIDE? (IF THEY DO CHANGE THE EVENT, IT'S MOST LIKELY NOT IN YOUR FAVOR.)

If you act like the first firefighter in your relationships, at work, with your family, friends, when you are playing a sport, watching a sport, or even at a funeral...you should fire yourself. You'll live a better life and probably save it in the long run!

When the mind no longer manipulates you, when the mind no longer controls you, when the mind is just a mechanism — if you need, you use it, otherwise you put it aside — you are free of the mind, you have attained your own masterhood.

~Osho

It's Cool To Know You Are Kinda Worthless!

I want you to do something for me. Go to the kitchen, get a sharp knife and cut your arm above your elbow. Okay... DON'T DO THAT. But if you did cut yourself, what does your body do to heal itself?

How does it know to get the molecules and all the glob and gook in that particular area to fix what it needs to? Your body will even make a scab to protect it! What was your part in it?

NOT MUCH!

You just sit there like a fool and tell your friends how cool your cut was and if you got it from a ski trip maybe laugh about it and share it. Besides that, you are just a bystander of your body. Kinda cool, right?

What do you do when you get hungry? Do you set an alarm to let your body know it's time to eat? Does someone remind you that it's time to eat? Well, maybe your mom does, but that's because she loves you. I promise you that if she wasn't around, your body knows the exact time when it needs to eat. Hell, it'll even tell you when you need to drink water and make a poopy! What was your part in it?

NOT MUCH!

While you're reading this, your mouth is salivating making sure your mouth is clean, your eyes are shutting making sure you're getting moisture, and your skin is shedding, but not too fast, just enough for new skin to come in. What was your part in it?

NOT MUCH!

Your brain does brain things, like have a billion thoughts per second. It makes thoughts come and go without you doing anything. It will even make you feel anxious if it feels it needs to, it will make you feel happy if it needs to, it will give you adrenaline if it thinks you need it. You don't have to do anything. When you have thoughts come and go, like if you all of a sudden think about the hair on your arm or the chicken stuck between your teeth, what was your part in it?

NOT MUCH!

Okay, we've got that part down.

With the same logic, let's see what happens when we try to control those things.

If you cut yourself and keep rubbing it to help it out and keep getting it wet to keep it clean and keep telling everyone how painful it is and start to cry, will it help?

NO!

Your body will heal itself on its own, so let it! You can cry, spit, and shout if you want to, but it really won't help!

If you're hungry, do you think that talking about it and running around crying about it will change it?

NO!

Your body will need what it needs (with your help, of course, or it will really tell you it's hungry and maybe even get pissed off and pass out).

You can cry, spit, and shout if you want to, but it really won't help!

Your brain will think thoughts all day! If you think that trying to control them and trying to grasp ideas in your mind that have no bearing on what you do with them will help, it really won't. It's going to do what it's going to do.

You can cry, spit, and shout if you want to about events in the world. You can get pissed off at something for a day, or a minute, or a second. It won't matter. The feeling you want to create and make into something is all your own doing.

Once your body is done with the adrenaline of the event, whatever you decide to do with the feeling after that is up to you.

It's like if you are starving and you are finally full, if you want to still let everyone know that you are upset that you were starving a few days ago, by all means you can, but at that point, your body is done feeling hungry and it's YOU deciding to put any effort into your shitty feeling.

Don't blame it on your stomach, and don't blame it on your thoughts. Your brain has already gone through a million other thoughts. If you want to decide to stay on one particular thought and give it power, please do. Keep in mind that a thought is immaterial and has no real value, power, or weight! It's NOTHING...until you make it into something. Yes! You create the feeling with the thought you decide to hold on to. I just think it's silly and it really won't serve a purpose. You can just let that thought pass through, just like the thought you may have had about what to eat tonight...they both carry the same weight! (Except you think the THOUGHT about the fight with your girlfriend means more.)

NOPE!

Although the THOUGHT may seem more important, I know that the thought is just this immaterial thing passing through. And when I see a thought for what it is, I don't do what most miserable couples do...brew in that stupid thought for hours, days, or even months as if it has anything good to offer me.

Don't believe me?

Talk to couples who are doing great!

Are they thinking about much?

NOPE.

They are just having fun...two kids in a playground...two people dancing the dance of love...two lovebirds singing the song of mushy things lovers sing...

Talk to couples who are doing shitty...

They are in their thoughts, aren't they?

They call their friends, and stay in their thoughts...they wake up in the middle of the night, awakened from their thoughts...they try to work out to forget their THOUGHTS!

There is nothing REAL that they are upset about...they just

think the thought has power, strength, and get this...some sort of wisdom!

HA HA!

FOOLS! (It's just a thought, might I add...)

Anyway....

Look, things in life will appear good and things in life will appear to look negative.

Nothing new!

I've realized that giving more thinking to an event will not make the event better or worse. It just gives it more thinking.

Let your brain do what it does and don't try to interrupt the natural order of your body by jumping in and adding your two cents (also known as your thoughts).

Yes, you are getting in your own way by adding grief, self-punishment, anger and all the other crap about your life that you think will actually make a difference by doing the rain dance.

You can cry, scream, shout, get pissed off, punch a wall, spit...if you want. The event will still be the event, with or without you crying, spitting, shouting about it.

YOU CAN CRY, SPIT or SHOUT IF YOU WANT, BUT IT REALLY WON'T HELP!

That's just not how the system works.

(Once you see that, you can remove the job of crying, spitting and shouting and let your body and mind do their natural thing — help you get out of your own way.)

The art of resting the mind and the power of dismissing from it all care and worry is probably one of the secrets of energy in our great men.

~Captain J.A. Hadfield

Q: Three people work at a used car dealership. Which is the Correct Answer?

The first Guy says, "I have the worst job! My job keeps me down, the people that come to see me don't respect me and nothing seems to ever change in my life!"

The second guy says, "I have the best life in the world. I am alive, I get to go to work and make people happy, I get to mingle with the customers and go home and do it all over again!"

The third guy says, "Look at both of these guys; they have thoughts and they live their lives. Sucks for the first guy for allowing his thoughts about the outside world to make himself feel so bad.

Awesome for the second guy to have such a great outlook about his life. I will just sit back and know that sometimes my thoughts will make me feel like I have good days, and sometimes my thoughts will make me think I am having bad days. But more importantly, they are just thoughts and they will only gain momentum and strength if I want to give it to them. In other words, I won't hold on to any particular thought and just let my mind do what it wants. That way, I can have one less job to think about and I can go back to work at my used car dealership...

I have discovered that all of man's unhappiness derives from only one source, not being able to sit quietly in a room.

~Blaise Pascal

A questionnaire asked the Sage, Sri Nisargadatta Maharaj, how to get the wisdom to be free of all and any worries and sorrow of our own thoughts. Here is the dialogue:

Question: How do I get it?

Maharaj: You need not get at it, for you *are* it. It will get at you if you give it a chance. Let go your attachment to the unreal and the real will swiftly and smoothly step into its own. Stop imagining yourself being or doing this or that and the realization that you are the source and heart of all will dawn upon you. With this will come great love which is not choice or predilection, nor attachment, but a power which makes all things love-worthy and lovable.

(From the book *I AM THAT*)

There is no 'how' to be free.

If you ask 'how' to be free, you are not listening.

~ J. Krishnamurti

What Are You Looking For?

This old story is one that has been shared many times over, but I think in this context it might be useful to hear again:

A man is on his hands and knees, looking for something under a lamppost and obviously not finding it. The neighborhood policeman asks what he is doing.

"I'm looking for my keys."

"Did you lose them around here?"

"Not exactly; I think I left them on the kitchen table at my house."

"Then why aren't you looking for them at your house?"

"The light is better over here."

You may have noticed that everything in this book relates to one central idea. It's not a "thing" to do or figure out. It's not a three-step system or a new approach to substitute your old one with. Matter of fact, it's just an insight. I do not want you to make this a "thing" to do. If you make this a thing to do or figure out, you might as well try to find it by the light on the lamppost.

The answer to well-being is that you already have it. Your default state, although it may not seem like it, is that you already have well-being. The only way to screw it up is not to believe this and try to find it outside yourself...

Do you know why most of us look outside of ourselves to go find it?

Because it's easier to see things outside of ourselves. We can buy physical books, attend physical seminars, talk to a physical coach or therapist, and watch physical videos about all the secrets to happiness. The problem is, the happiness you're trying to achieve is already inside of you. It's hard to grasp because it has no form...just like memories. And just like memories, although they don't really exist anymore, it can feel just as real as the actual experience. So it makes sense to look outside of yourself to find the answer! YOU CAN SEE THE OUTSIDE WORLD.

But just because the outside world looks more comprehensible doesn't mean that's where you will find it. Just because the light is shining where the drunk guy is looking for his keys, doesn't mean that's where he will find them. The light might look brighter there and it may be easier to see, but I assure you, you're looking in the wrong place.

So, here is the question: How do you go looking

for happiness if it's already inside of you? I'm not sure. It's like my dad, who used to look for his eyeglasses for 20 minutes when they were on his head the whole time! How would you tell my dad that he can stop looking? I guess the only thing you can really do is point to his head. Once he realizes the glasses are on his head, it would be kind of pointless to keep telling him they're anywhere else. But that's what people have gotten you to believe — that happiness is on the outside.

IT'S NOT!

Here is the other problem. As soon as we start to believe that happiness is the default state of our lives, we try not looking for it, which is the other side of the coin. It's like the person who tells you not to think of a pink elephant.

So, this game starts to happen. What do we do? Do we look for it, not look for it, forget about it, understand it, or just give up?

What I do know is that as soon as you see it, there is no other way to explain it. And as soon as I explain it, there is no way to see it!

I didn't make up the rules, the rules were already there. I just happen to finally see how the rules work. Once you see the rules, the funny thing is, it will start working for you, too...

INSTANT ENLIGHTENMENT!
(The Answer is in the box!)

A RIDDLE YOU MAY ALREADY HAVE THE ANSWER TO...

You go out and talk to this person that you've met a bunch of times.

You tell your friend about this person but... but...wait...what was his name again?

You start to remember what he wore, where you met him, where you met him the time before. You even recall the exact conversation.

But WHAT WAS HIS NAME?

Let me ask you...what do you do to remember this person's name?

(Hint: it's not when you try to use your knowledge, is it?)

NOPE!

It's when you get up to pee at 3:00 a.m. or when you're in the shower or when...
YOU'RE NOT THINKING ABOUT IT and
WHEN YOU'RE NOT TRYING TO FORCE IT!

YUP!

Your brain is really funny! When you try really hard, it doesn't want to help you.

When you let it go...*voilà!* It miraculously shows up! (It's actually not miraculous, it's just the way our brains work!)

So, the next time you can't figure something out...want to know what to do?

NOTHING!

From Nothing...Something will emerge! It's just the way it works!

"The moment I think or say something, I know that the opposite of what I think or say could also be true. Then the opposites are no longer at war. Then they complement each other rather than threaten each other. Then you get to *play* with the opposites.

Then life becomes playful, and words are no longer the enemy."

~Jeff Foster, *An Extraordinary Absence*

WHAT ABOUT THE PAST OR THE FUTURE?

Your memories and the future are happening this very exact moment you are thinking about it!

You have to think about the past NOW to see it!

You have to think about the future NOW to create it.

The past and the present can only be comprehended in this moment of thought. They don't exist anywhere else...

The past and future aren't there. It's just what's happening now. The way to see either of them is NOW. THAT'S IT!

You are the moment. There is nothing you can do about it. That's a good thing.

To suffer the past...you have to remember the past NOW and create the bad feelings in this moment! Your feelings aren't stored anywhere! You have to create the grief and pain NOW!

To suffer in the future...you have to create the future NOW and engineer the bad feelings in this moment! The pain does not live in some future place waiting for you to catch it like a germ. You have to create it NOW!

So, if you want to grieve about the past, bring up the feelings NOW and make yourself feel like shit. If you want to worry about the future, then think about the future NOW and make yourself feel like shit. Remember one crucial thing: you have to create those memories now. They really don't exist until you fabricate them. I sometimes fabricate them, but I don't let them take a hold of me. It's kind of cool to know that it's just a screen in my mind, with no real power. Kind of like a dream. There is something special that happens when you realize that. The feelings from the past and the horrid thoughts of the future just don't mean as much.

"Sometimes the questions are complicated and the answers are simple."

~Dr. Seuss

This is the situation of your head: I see cycle-handles and pedals and strange things that you have gathered from everywhere.

Such a small head...and no space to live in! And that rubbish on moving in your head; your head goes on spinning and weaving – it keeps you occupied. Just think what kind of thoughts go inside of your mind.

One day just sit, close your doors, and write down for half an hour whatsoever is passing in your mind, and you will understand what I mean and you will be surprised what goes on inside your mind. It remains in the background, it is constantly there, it surrounds you like a cloud.

With this cloud you cannot know reality; you cannot attain to spiritual perception. This cloud has to be dropped. And it is just with your decision to drop it that it will disappear. You are clinging to it – the cloud is not interested in you, remember it.

***The Sun Rises in the Evening*, Chapter 9, by Osho**

Your Shoes are Not the Problem

I had a coaching client who wanted to figure out how she would know when she met the right partner.

I told her well, if there are two guys you met at a bar and you have chemistry with one and not the other, how would you know?

She started to tell me all the reasons, then paused for a moment and said, "Actually, you just know."

I said perfect, there is your answer.

That wasn't good enough, so she told me that there is this guy she should really like because he is good to her, her family and friends, and he has a steady job and everything else, but there is no chemistry. She asked me what the problem was.

So I told her: "If he were in a room with another guy and you wanted to find out if you had chemistry with one of them, how would you know?"

I think she got the point. No matter how much we try to bullet-point good or bad things about our relationships, our family, business, and ourselves, our desires and internal understanding will always trump our knowledge. We can try to remove the desire, but you know desire always creeps back. Most of us will skirt desire out of the way by rationalizing it and giving it meaning.

Desire is a desire, with or without your input.

Does that mean that your desire is always right? Not necessarily, but it's a great starting point to listen to its insights.

If someone came to me and said, "I don't know what my problem is, I keep falling and I've done so many things to help prevent it."

I would ask, what things?

"Well, I changed my shoe size, I changed the color of my shoes and I even bought Hi-Tops. With all the changes, I still can't keep myself from falling!"

What if you're looking in the wrong place?

"I can't be! I went to a shoe specialist who has written books on falling and he even recommended these special shoes that have a wide sole that help prevent people from falling. It worked for a few weeks, but last night, I didn't see a curb and I tripped again! I'm going to his seminar to see if he has any new ideas about what shoes I need to get. I even have a shoe therapist I visit once a week who looks at my shoes and offers me advice on them. I become more aware of my steps, but I still fall from time to time."

What do you think could help this situation? What if she knew how gravity worked? Do you think this would help?

YES!

You see, as soon as she sees that it's not the shoe, its color, or its size; that it's just the way the laws work, spending precious time on the shoes just becomes a pointless endeavor.

If she realizes that gravity pushes people down, no matter the shoe, she can go on with her life knowing what's causing her fall. Matter of fact, her focusing on her shoes was distracting her from finding the real answer. She was looking in the wrong place!

As long as we find the law that runs her problem, the answer is pretty easy to find.

Most people create a shoe problem.

The person asking how she will know when she has chemistry was creating a shoe problem. The law of attraction is very simple. You feel it or you don't. Any other response to the question is going to distract your body's own ability to answer the question. You're essentially creating a shoe problem to find out why you are falling. Matter of fact, if you realize and listen to the law of chemistry, which starts as a feeling, an intuition, and an insight, it just may give you the answer you are looking for.

Does that mean that once you know how gravity works, you're not going to fall?

Absolutely not!

It just means that you don't have to look for answers in the wrong place anymore!

Does that mean that by listening to your intuition and really putting some trust in your intuition, it is always going to be right?

Absolutely not!

It just means that you don't have to look for the answers in the wrong place anymore and that you may just find the answer you're looking for a bit quicker.

"Trust your own instinct. Your mistakes might as well be your own, instead of someone else's."
~Billy Wilder

EXERCISE #233

If you have a brilliant idea, a thought, or just want to clear your mind and put something into words, which canvas would you think would be better to write on?

- A) A canvas that already has a bunch of scribbles, old ideas, prejudices, fears, judgments, noise and disturbances?

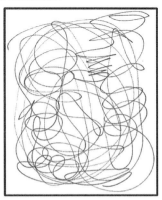

- B) Or a canvas that has NO preconceived notions, scribbles, old ideas, prejudices, fears, judgments, noise or disturbances?

_____

Question: If you want to know whether the job, relationship, future, understanding, marriage, love, resolution, question, problem, issue, or anything else for that matter, needs to be re-evaluated, do you think the canvas in your brain would do a better job with scribbles already on it, or one with NO pre-conceived notions, scribbles, old ideas, prejudices, fears, judgments, noise or disturbances?

Answer Here: _____

(If you know the answer already, then stop doing it the old way!)

Some Wise Words:

Many of our problems — perhaps most of our problems — are because we never look at them face-to-face, encountered them. And not looking at them is giving them energy. Being afraid of them is giving them energy, always trying to avoid them is giving energy — because you are accepting that they are real. Your very acceptance is their existence. Other than your acceptance, they don't really exist.

~Osho

A Christian, a psychologist and a Muslim see the ocean for the first time.

The Christian says, "Wow, God is good! Look at the beauty that God has created with His wisdom and powers. He has given us all of this so we can live in peace and harmony with the plants, animals, and the universe! Look at the design and beauty of the ocean! God is good!"

The psychologist says, "Well, the strongest connection between the nature experiences and individuals' feelings about themselves is that they feel comfortable in their natural surroundings and are surprised at how easily this sense of belonging has developed. There is a growing sense of wonder and a complex awareness of spiritual and self-created meanings as individuals feel at one with nature, yet they are aware of the transience of individual concerns when seen against the background of enduring natural rhythms."

The Muslim says, "Wow, Allah is good! Look at the beauty that Allah has created with his wisdom and powers. He has given us all of this so we can live in peace and harmony with the plants, animals, and the universe! Look at the design and beauty of the ocean! Allah is good!"

As the three were pondering the ocean and its beauty, a simple man walked over to them to see what all the fuss was about. The three men looked over and asked the simple man why the ocean seemed beautiful.

The simple man simply said, "It's beautiful because it just is."

All the other wise men looked at him and scoffed at the simple man. Obviously, the simple man was too simple to understand beauty. So, the three wise men went right back to explaining beauty the way they saw it, while the simple man enjoyed the beauty of the ocean...

Losing an illusion makes you wiser than finding a truth.
~Zen Quote

Existence is not a problem to be solved, it is a mystery to be lived. And you should be perfectly aware what the difference is between a mystery and a problem.

A problem is something created by the mind; a mystery is simply there, not created by the mind. A problem has ugliness in it, like a disease. A mystery is beautiful. With a problem, immediately a fight arises. You have to solve it; something is wrong, you have to put it right; something is missing, you have to supply the missing link. With mystery there is no question of that.

The moon rises in the night...it is not a problem, it is a mystery. You have to live with it. You have to dance with it, you have to sing with it, or you can just be silent with it. Something mysterious surrounds you.

~Osho

If we have not quiet in our minds, outward comfort will do no more for us than a golden slipper on a gouty foot.

~John Bunyan

If you are a Buddhist, Mormon, Atheist, Christian, Baptist, Psychologist, Musician, Artist, Mother, Homeless, Estranged Husband, Child, Murderer, Savior, Lover, Veterinarian, Veteran, Feminist, Author, or anything else that you can label yourself as...

The world on the outside; the trees, cars, animals, leaves, sky, air, swings, clouds and everything else are doing what they do, no matter which person's eyes you decide to see them from.

The only difference is when you look at it from a Buddhist, Mormon, Atheist, Christian, Baptist, Psychologist, Musician, Artist, Mother, Homeless, Estranged Husband, Child, Murderer, Savior, Lover, Veterinarian, Veteran, Feminist, Author, or anybody else's point of view...

The outside world; the trees, cars, animals, leaves, sky, air, swings, clouds and everything else are going to look completely different.

Who is right? What if you stepped back and didn't see the world as anything but what it is. How would the world look then? I know it's hard to do. But it's so damn liberating in the end...

The world outside does not care at all about the person who is looking at it. The person we are inside of our heads gives the illusion that if we care in our own way, it somehow changes the outside world.

But the truth of the matter is, the outside world is neither Buddhist, Mormon, Atheist, Christian, Baptist,

Psychologist, Musician, Artist, Mother, Homeless, Estranged Husband, Child, Murderer, Savior, Lover, Veterinarian, Veteran, Feminist, Author, or anything else.

The outside world? It just is. Once you grasp that, the paradigm of reality gets shifted. To what? To insights, life, energy, gifts and resources that we never saw because we only saw the world as a Buddhist, Mormon, Atheist, Christian, Baptist, Psychologist, Musician, Artist, Mother, Homeless, Estranged Husband, Child, Murderer, Savior, Lover, Veterinarian, Veteran, Feminist, Author, or anything else we artificially conceived.

If you think you have the truth, you can be absolutely sure of one thing…that you think that you have the truth.

~Amir Karkouti

Mental Illness vs. Mental Well-Being

"People Consenting to the Labels and The Regulations of a System are Bound by Their Agreements"

So, what is the difference between someone who is in the mental illness profession and the work that I do?

Before I begin, I'd like to make it clear; I am not degreed or giving medical advice. I am just some guy who has helped a lot of people with some ideas that may resonate with the reader.

When we come from a certain psychological place — i.e., fear, anger, curiosity etc. — we tend to come up with different answers to solutions depending on the feeling or space we are in at the moment. In other words, if Hitler has an idea for world peace vs. Gandhi, I think we will both agree, based on where they are gathering their answers, they will both have radically different solutions to world peace.

With that being said, I do believe that people who are working in the mental illness profession and I are both looking for solutions to relieve or remove anxiety, depression and/or low moods. The only difference is how we look at a client will dramatically change how we will come to a solution.

The DSM-5 development website proposes the following new definition of mental disorder (APA, 2012):

1. A behavioral or psychological syndrome or pattern that occurs in an individual
2. That reflects an underlying psychobiological dysfunction
3. The consequences of which are clinically significant distress (e.g., a painful symptom) or disability (i.e., impairment in one or more important areas of functioning)
4. Must not be merely an expectable response to common stressors and losses (for example, the loss of a loved one) or a culturally sanctioned response to a particular event (for example, trance states in religious rituals)
5. That is not primarily a result of social deviance or conflicts with society

At first, this may seem like an ordinary definition of mental disorders. But upon close examination, we can see there may be a few fundamental flaws as to how this may lead to the wrong solution.

The first issue from the above definition is: How do we truly distinguish what a mental disorder is or isn't? The first definition also implies that it's a "syndrome or pattern" that occurs "IN" an individual. The assumption here is that it's something that is happening inside of us. It assumes it's something that we have and need to get rid of.

The second definition further assumes the "something" that is happening inside of us is a psychobiological dysfunction. In other words, this thing that we have inside of us is biological. In theory, we would be able to test this using biological markers or testers. Ask anyone who is going through anxiety or low moods what types of markers and testers are used in order to diagnose them properly. You'll soon find that it's not too convincing. And rightfully so, considering the answers they are looking for are coming from asking the wrong questions.

The idea behind someone who has a mental illness is to treat the symptom via cognitive behavior therapy, drugs, or prevention if possible.

When we see clients or patients as having a mental illness, it only makes sense to try to resolve their issue toward mental well-being.

What if we could see it from another point of view? What if we could integrate what we have learned from psychology and the mental fields and integrate with a big piece of the puzzle that is either disregarded or misunderstood; to improve the lives of so many who don't need to live in the state in which they are presently living.

What if we saw clients as having complete mental well-being, and the reason for their issue is not that they are sick or have an illness — rather, it is that they are looking at their problem incorrectly, which will lead to an incorrect answer. How would answers look then?

My fundamental approach to helping a client is to make them aware that they have perfect health, and that they are not seeing their issues because they are too clouded in their thinking, which is creating that particular reality they want to get rid of. Once they realize they have perfect health and that they are simply not seeing it, it opens up a door to a solution so simple that it's often missed.

I'd like to use a simple metaphor to illustrate my point.

A client comes to a mental illness professional and says that they are holding a cup where all their mental well-being resides, but it's completely empty. So, the natural response is to find out why their cup is empty, when it started to become empty, and find ways to fill it back up so the cup is full of happiness, love, and well-being. Sometimes that is done through sessions with a mental illness professional; sometimes it's done using drugs or cognitive behavior therapy and modification. Ultimately, the goal is to fill up their cup of well-being so it is full again.

If they get bouts where they are losing their well-being again, the professional's job is to find out why the cup is draining and what they can do together to fill it up again. The paradigm of this type of work is to notice when the cup is draining and find ways to refill it using tools, strategies, and/or behavior modification.

When a client comes into my office and says their cup of mental well-being is empty and they need to fill it up, my first conversation is about how cups may seem to look empty, but everyone's cup is always full. Some people imagine it as empty and they start to believe it; some people hallucinate that the cup is empty and they start to believe it; and some people are so engrossed in the thought of the cup being empty that they start to believe it.

So, if we start with the premise that their cup is full to begin with, we don't spend the rest of the time trying to figure out why their cup is empty and instead focus on finding out why they are not seeing their cup as full. It becomes a fundamental paradigm change in their understanding of their condition.

Once the window is slightly cracked open and the possibility of them being perfect is explored, the exploration becomes one that makes the search not only positive, but also heartfelt.

There is a certain ring to everyone that they know they are perfect. Even the ones who don't believe they are know that there is something wrong with them or they wouldn't feel the need to be treated. We all have a fundamental understanding when we are off in our thinking. It takes someone who is whole and perfect in my eyes to see this. Even the ones who don't see it right away, as soon as we start from a place of mental well-being and the issue of not seeing that well-being, you'd be surprised how many people open up to that possibility.

I am not here to say that this is a 100 percent, foolproof way of doing change work. There are times that people are so low or down in their mood, their head is so clouded, that a professional needs to medicate or put them in a place where they don't hurt themselves or others. After the initial dust settles, the better approach is to show them, even in the worst state, that they are perfect and that they veered away from being perfectly whole because of the thinking they had in the moment. Trying to find out why their cup seems empty when it's full the whole time will lead to a long road of irrelevant questions, solutions, and even in the worst case, more cups having been created in their thoughts that may now need more ways to fill up.

The question *Is your cup half full or half empty?* has finally been answered. It's neither. Your cup is always full, it's just a matter of whether you are in a moment where you THINK your cup is half empty or half full. The reality is, your cup is ALWAYS full; just be open to that possibility and new doors will emerge. They have to.

Bring Your Snow Globe With You

I want you to imagine a snow globe. I want you to imagine that the water inside the globe is your thinking. I want you to imagine that the flakes inside the snow globe are your thoughts.

If I asked you what you would need to do to settle the flakes, to allow clear thinking, what would you say?

Think about it?

Would you even have to do anything?

Actually, quite the opposite. In order to settle the flakes, the only thing you'd have to do is just...

LEAVE IT ALONE!

But it can't be that easy! We have so many thoughts in our heads! We must do something!

Well, if you call doing nothing, doing something, than by all means do something!

But make sure to do nothing first!

To settle the storm in the snow globe, the only thing you can do is set it aside. Leave it alone! Stop playing with it!

Your well-being works the same way when you set your thoughts aside, and your thinking clears up without you doing anything! The natural state of your thinking's well-being happens when you become aware of this. It's that simple.

So why do people go on vacation? To let the water in their thinking globe settle. They think it's Hawaii doing it. It's not. They just allow themselves to put their mental globe aside so they can mentally "rest." And it's funny how we come up with so many creative ideas when we are on vacation. I know that vacation is not what allows people to relax mentally. Why do I know that? Because I know many friends and family members who bring their snow globes with them to their vacation and shake the shit out of them! And you know that they are not resting, even when they are on vacation.

So, why do people go to church? To allow the water in their thinking globe to settle. They think it's church that's doing it. But it's not. They just allow themselves to put their mental snow globe aside so they can mentally rest and be closer to God. I know that it's not church that allows people to mentally relax. Why do I know this? Because I know many friends and family members who bring their mental snow globes to church and shake the shit out of them. And you know that they are not resting, even when they are at church.

So, why do people go to the beach, coffee shop, bookstore, yoga class, bedroom, movie theater, etc.? To allow the water in their thinking globe to settle. They think it's the beach, coffee shop, bookstore, yoga class, bedroom, or movie theater that's doing it. I know that it's not the beach, coffee shop, bookstore, yoga class, bedroom, or movie theater that allows people to mentally relax. Why do I know this? Because I know many friends and family members who bring their mental snow globes to the beach, coffee shop, book store, yoga class, bedroom, and movie theater and shake the shit out of them. And you know that they are not resting, even when they are at the beach, coffee shop, bookstore, yoga class, bedroom, or movie theater.

So what's the common denominator?

You can be anywhere in the world, *anywhere*...and be relaxed and in a state of well-being. All you have to do is put your snow globe down!

It's that simple. When you put your snow globe down, the flakes naturally settle, allowing your water (mind) to clear. There is nothing more you need to do.

Matter of fact, if you try to do something, you will need to pick up the snow globe in order to do it. And as soon as you do that, you are stirring the globe again. You can't settle thinking by thinking. It just doesn't work. That's like trying to not shake the snow globe by shaking it. It doesn't make sense for the snow globe. It won't make sense for your well-being.

So put your snow globe down and do nothing. Once you do that, the possibilities, insights, and aha moments will come from a place that you never thought possible. Have a little faith, trust in yourself. Settling your thoughts is the only way you have to clear thinking and mental well-being.

Any time you feel your head going a thousand miles per minute, remember to put your snow globe down, and your innate wisdom will do the rest. Don't try to do anything. That's what got you into trouble in the first place!

"SNOW AGAIN, TODAY..."

Your Train of Thought

In 1896 approximately 10 people were invited to what we now call a movie screening. But in 1896 the people who were witnessing this screening would see something that they had never seen before.

Anxiously waiting, the people in town sat down and looked at a white screen. The directors, two brothers, Auguste and Louis Lumiere, were excited to show their new motion picture called *The Arrival of a Train at La Ciotat Station.*

Keep in mind that at that point people had never seen a movie before, let alone a movie that would show a locomotive heading toward them.

The movie pops up on the screen and lo and behold, according to urban legend, everyone panics, jumps up from their chairs, and runs out of the room!

Since they had never seen a movie before, they believed that what was on the screen was actually real. The audience members literally believed that a train was heading their way.

If you see the movie now you would laugh to think that it would scare anyone. But when you don't know how things like projectors work, your brain will do the best it can to comprehend what's going on. If you had never seen a train on a flat screen before and it was heading toward you, you'd also most likely run out of the room.

You're probably wondering what this has to do with you.

This story has a lot to do with you.

Matter of fact, this is how most people live their lives. The parallel of not knowing how the movie screen projects light and how the mind projects our reality is uncanny.

The people in the theater were escorted back and the directors went on to explain that what they had seen on the screen was not real.

It was simply light reflected on the projection screen, which created the illusion of an actual train.

As soon as they understood the mechanics of the projector, they were able to relax and enjoy the movie.

Most people don't understand how our thinking works.

Most of us never had a director to tell them that the movie in their head is just a projection of their reality.

It's not real reality. In other words, what you see in the outside world cannot be directly experienced! Reality as you see it get's filtered through your eyes, ears, nose, touch, taste, balance, etc. Your brain, by design, cannot grasp all of reality. It can only grab the parts "it" thinks are relevant at the moment. That explains why when you are in a rush and you're looking for your keys that are right in front of you, you miss them!

So, what do most of us do instead? We go on doing what others believe works. They pass down ideas for inner peace from others who believe they know how to obtain it. We come up with theories, ideas, and assumptions to make ourselves happy. But is that the answer?

I want you to go back in time and imagine it's 1896. You're returning back to your seats after the initial scare of the train coming toward you on the screen.

Imagine that the director believes the best way to calm you down is to simply change the movie to something nicer — something more relaxing.

Let's say that instead of a train arriving he puts a video of fluffy little bunnies on the screen so it won't look as scary. The bunny video would definitely calm the nerves more than a video of a train. The problem is, what do we do when we see a train video again?

Many of us live our lives trying to change the scenery instead of understanding the mechanisms of how our thinking works.

We simply change the picture in hopes of having a better reality.

That may work and it does for many, but a lot of times it lasts only as long as we have a good movie playing in our heads. At that point, we have to succumb to what's playing in our heads. That does not give us any option for our inner peace. Our peace becomes dictated by the movie that's playing. I know that's not how I'd like to live my life.

What if we didn't have to change the movie (your thoughts) in your head?

What if somebody told you how movies work and that

is just not that real? What if you realized that your thoughts are just formless projections that don't really have any power, any rhyme or reason, no way of being controlled? What if they are just happenings? Would it even make sense to try to control them?

Sure, some thoughts feel like they mean more than others. But who's giving them power? Who is bringing these thoughts to light?

Do you think it's better to change the movie on the screen to make you feel better, or is it better to know how projectors work, so the next time you see a movie you're not startled?

If you're like me, you'd probably say that you'd like to know how projectors worked. After all, changing the movie just changed the movie. Knowing the behind the scenes of how the light put the movie on the screen would give you a bit more understanding, would it not?

Not only would it save you the time and trouble to look for a better movie (or better thought, a calmer place to remove your thoughts, etc.) you'll soon realize you won't need movies at all to make you feel better.

I'm going to let you in on a secret; the reality is that the thoughts that come through your head are no different than the light projecting the images on a screen. If you don't have this little understanding, it can be very frightening indeed.

Many of us see a projected thought in our mind and allow the formless thought to gain power. We must understand, like the train arriving on the screen, it has no real power.

It's just a thought and that's all it is!

The reason that positive thinking affirmations don't last long is the very same reason trying to change the movie on the screen will not be the answer to long-lasting inner peace. Understanding the mechanism of the projector, and the mechanism that your thoughts really don't hold much power, is transformative!

Being aware that your thoughts are just thoughts is all that you need to know.

They are just thoughts. They hold no power unless you plug it into your reality. A power saw can't do anything unless it's plugged in. It's that simple.

Be aware. You will have over 70,000 thoughts a day without your control and the only ones that will have any power over you are the ones that you give power to.

They need you as much as you think you need them.

In actuality, you really don't need them at all (at least in the sense of giving them power).

What I mean by that is, when you let them just fly by your head like a movie reel they don't do much but keep your brain occupied. They have a purpose. It's just that we've been fooled to think that their purpose is for us to control them!

I know that as soon as I take one of those thoughts and allow it to consume me, it can feel pretty damn real. I also know that when I remember that it's just a thought and at any moment that thought can turn into a completely new one, it just doesn't have the power it once used to.

Isn't it funny that solutions tend to show up when we're not occupied with looking for the answer.

Sometimes, doing NOTHING will lead to the SOMETHING...that you've been looking for!

~Amir Karkouti

Question (Roderick) - Beloved Master, I am sitting silently doing nothing, and the weeds are growing all around me.

Osho - Roderick, weeds are divine. Don't call them weeds. They are as spiritual as the Buddhas. They partake of God as much as roses. Remove men from the earth -- will there be any difference between weeds and roses? All these distinctions are made up by the mind.

You are not really sitting silently; otherwise, who is telling you weeds are growing? Your mind is still functioning, whispering things to you. It is your mind! If you are really silent there is no mind -- then whether weeds grow or roses grow it is all the same to you. What difference is there? Can't you enjoy weeds? They are beautiful people! See the weeds swaying, dancing in the wind, in the sun.... What do you think is lacking in them which roses have? Nothing is lacking. This is just an idea, and ideas change. It is possible one day that roses may go out of fashion, weeds may become an "in" thing.

A hundred years ago nobody had ever thought that cactuses would be loved by people, but now the cactus is "in" and the rose is "out." To talk about the rose looks old-fashioned, looks orthodox, conventional; to talk about cactuses is avant-garde, it shows that you are modern, contemporary. People are keeping cactuses in their bedrooms -- dangerous cactuses, poisonous cactuses, which can kill you! But they have come into fashion, and once something comes into fashion there are so many fools who start appreciating it.

People simply go on following whatsoever is made fashionable by a few clever and cunning people. Just a hundred years ago nobody would have liked Picasso's paintings, and now Picasso is the greatest artist -- not only of this century but of the whole history. What has happened? Just the fashion has changed. People get tired of one thing; they go on moving to the opposite extreme.

Roderick, there is nothing wrong in weeds! There is nothing wrong in anything. The idea of right and wrong means the mind is there. You are not sitting silently and you are not sitting doing nothing. You are discriminating, and that is action. You are labeling, and that is thinking. And you are judging. Drop all judgment, all labeling, all discrimination... and just watch weeds growing. So what -- let them grow! When you don't have a mind at all, you are also a weed; so weeds growing around you, it is not something strange -- weeds surrounding a weed! Enjoy!

Once a Zen master was asked by a king -- because the master was a great painter -- to paint a picture of a bamboo.

The master said, "It will take time."

"How long?" asked the king.

The master said, "That is difficult to say, but at least two or three years."

The king said, "Are you mad or something? You are one of the greatest painters. I was thinking you could just draw it right now!"

He said, "That is not the problem, drawing a bamboo is not the problem -- but first I have to be a bamboo;

otherwise how do I know what a bamboo is? I want to know the bamboo from the inside! So I will have to go and live in a bamboo grove. Now, one never knows how long it will take. Unless I know the bamboo from within I cannot paint it. That has been my practice my whole life: I paint only that which I have known from its deepest core."

The king said, "Okay, I will wait."

One year passed. He sent a few people to see what was happening, whether the man was alive or dead. They came back and said, "The man is alive, but we don't think that he is a man anymore -- he is a bamboo! He was swaying with the bamboos in the wind. We passed by his side; he didn't take any notice. We said, 'Hello!' He didn't hear. We wanted to talk to him. We looked at his eyes -- they were so empty that we became frightened; either he has gone mad or something has happened. And he can do anything, so we escaped. He may kill or, who knows? -- he may jump upon us! He is no more the same man."

The king himself went to see, and the master was swaying in the wind, in the sun. And the king asked, "Sir, what about my painting?" He didn't answer.

After three years he appeared at the court and he said, "Now bring the canvas and the paints. I am ready. And why were you people disturbing me again and again? If you had not disturbed me I would have come a little earlier. These fools from your court, they were saying things to me. They were saying, 'Hello!' Do you say hello to a bamboo? They disturbed the whole thing. It took months for me to again settle into being a bamboo and to forget that I am a man. And then you came and you said, 'Sir.' Is that the way to address a bamboo? 'When are you going to paint?' Has anybody ever heard that bamboos paint? You are a fool, you are surrounded by fools! I had told you that I would come whenever I was ready."

The canvas was brought, the brushes and the color, and within seconds he drew the bamboo. And it is said that the king wept for joy. He had never seen such a painting: it was so alive! It was no ordinary painting. It was not from the outside, it was from the bamboo -- as if a bamboo had sprouted on the canvas, not been painted.

Roderick, sit silently doing nothing, and let things happen -- whatsoever is happening. If weeds are growing, let them grow. They have the right to grow as much as you have the right to grow. And if you allow everything without any judgment, if you are nonjudgmental, you will grow to such pinnacles of joy and benediction that you cannot imagine right now.

Source - Osho Book *The Dhammapada, Vol. 11*

We cannot see our reflection in running water. It is only in still water that we can see.

~Taoist Proverb

Isn't it Just Interesting?

Isn't it just interesting that we seek the advice of coaches, therapists, and others outside of ourselves for clarity and answers?

What is it that they know that we don't know?

Isn't it interesting that WE can give sound advice to others about a particular situation, but if we encounter the same situation in our own lives, we are not so sure how to deal with it?

What is it that we know that others may not?

The truth of the matter is, neither the coach nor the advice of others is what is giving you the insight.

The real reason someone else sees it more clearly than you are seeing it is that they don't care as much as you do. They are putting less thought into your situation. The outcome to the person you're speaking to has less relevance in their lives, so they can give you a better answer.

That's the same reason why when you give advice to others, even if you've been in a similar situation, you can come up with better answers for them than you can for yourself.

This should tell you something. This should really tell you something BIG!

The reality is that you putting more relevance into your particular thinking for that particular situation DOES NOT MAKE IT BETTER! Matter of fact, as you know, the thinking and over-thinking about the situation is why you can't see the issue clearly in the first place.

If you need clarity or insights about a situation, I'm happy to say that you know exactly what you need to do. The only thing is, you need to get out of your own way to find it. If the person sitting next to you can give two shits about your problem, maybe you should "think" about it in the same manner. That doesn't make the circumstance unimportant. No, not at all. It makes your THINKING ABOUT IT less relevant.

We have this idea that when we are in a certain situation, if we think about it harder, or make our tummy hurt, it means more than if we just look at it like watering the plants. The reality is, both the "bad" situation or watering plants are the same thing. In reality, they are just events. The only difference between the events is the thinking, labeling, and idea we want to put into that event. Sure, you not getting the job sucks, but it doesn't suck as much to your neighbor because he hasn't really thought about it as much as you did. The funny thing is, he can probably help you out more than you can if you are now stuck in your thinking, SIMPLY BECAUSE HE'S NOT IN YOUR THINKING!

It's really that simple.

So, if you want to save time, money, and the drive to see someone who is willing to give you advice or clarity, just step back from your situation and realize that thinking about the event really just gives the event more thinking. As soon as you remove that job, a really interesting thing will start to happen...

You will get the exact insights, or even betters ones, that others were ready to give you, just because you've removed yourself from thinking about the problem. Knowing that the thinking is muddling your insights is all you need to know. This awareness brings you to seeing the event with a clear vision, a clean slate. The answer again is really to do nothing but see the event for what it is — simply an event.

Sure, if you want to tell me that you're event is more important than washing dishes, then I will show you someone who thinks washing dishes is more important than your event, whatever it may be. Between the two, I know that when I look at them as just events, I can make one more important than another just by adding my two cents of thought. It's really kind of pointless to add my thoughts to the event.

Try it out...or for that matter, don't try anything at all. Let me know what your inner coach comes up with.

"Inaction may be the highest form of action."
~Zen Proverb

While You're Busy Setting Goals…I'm Living My Life!

I was at a Tony Robbins-type event a few years back. It was during lunch when two divorced women were talking amongst themselves about how to find the ideal man.

The first woman asked the second woman if she had made her "Ideal Man" list. The second woman proudly went into her purse and pulled out a two-page list of what she wanted for her perfect mate! Two freakin' pages! Sixty bullet points describing her perfect mate, from appearance to outdoor activities. The first woman was so proud of her friend. After all, she finally had a concrete idea of her ideal mate. Doesn't that sound like a sensible thing to do?

A week ago, I had a roundtable discussion with a group of entrepreneurs about goal-setting and making vision boards for 2013.

They were so proud of the boards they'd made. I felt like I was in kindergarten again. The few wealthy people in the group looked at each other and said, "I'm confused. The guy is writing that he wants a Ferrari this year; I just set out to work and have fun in my Ferrari."

Hell, go open up your Facebook and you'll find

hundreds of people telling others to reach their goals, set their goals, and even ways to make their goals better by purchasing their product or going to their seminar.

Ahhh....Goals...Goals...Goals...

I have a confession to make...I've never really set goals...

I am doing just great!

Want to know another secret? I have never written down who my ideal woman is, nor what my ideal dinner or vacation would be.

I am doing just great!

What I am about to say may piss you off. I may even lose you as a friend on Facebook; however, that's not my goal (pun intended).

What I am about to tell you goes against the beliefs of everyone who is setting goals, making goals, or selling you on how to make or set goals.

I am even going against some of my teachers, mentors, and friends who have told me otherwise.

But here it goes...

For the most part...I have noticed that goals are for people who don't really want to do the thing that they set out to do.

Goals, for many, are things that they feel they need to create, because having the desire is not enough.

I am now on my 4th book without setting goals. I knew early on that I always wanted to write a book. Where does a goal fit in at that point?

If writing a book is something I desire, I either write one or don't.

All a goal would do is give me more thinking about my goal, vision board, or whatever, instead of…writing my book.

I have friends to this day who are talking about their goals to write their books; the goal of being a speaker, author, and sharing it with the world.

As they tell everyone about their goal, I'm busy writing my next chapter.

What I am saying is, goals have become noise for many to create a façade to make them feel like they should be doing what they are out to do. Goals have become the great "talking points" for the Tony Robbins followers and the like, to have a pow-wow; a connection to each other.

The ones who are doing the things they want to do…are doing the things they want to do.

Why?

Because they're doing the things they want to do.

Sounds so easy.

It is!

If you set out to do the things you want to do...

If you want to make it harder on yourself to do the things you want to do...

Set up goals and intricate goal calendars and plans to really give you more thinking about... well, doing the things you want to do...

So, are goals bad then?

NO.

For many, as you see on Facebook, the goal becomes the goal. Fulfilling the vision board or filling it up to look pretty on their wall becomes their compulsion. People become so pre-occupied with filling their thoughts and giving importance to the goal-setting, they forget about what they set out to do in the first place.

Going back to the lady who had her ideal mate's qualities written on paper, and what she NEEDS in a man, and spending the next three hours discussing the validity of her goals in a mate...I quietly smiled.

I know what I want in a woman, and do you know

why? Because I freakin' know what I want in a woman...it's that simple!

I don't write down what I want for breakfast, I don't write down why my best friend is my best friend, I don't write down why I don't like my neighbor's kids, because I know what I know. What makes you think that by over-thinking something you are going to get answers, or fulfill goals?

I wasn't going to bring studies into this idea, but studies have shown that people who set goals to lose weight and tell everyone that they are going to lose weight, end up not losing the weight because the idea of the goal and telling others about it became all that was needed for them to feel satisfied.**

For the non-goal-setters and people who don't need to write down who our ideal mates are...why are we just fine fulfilling what we want?

Because while you're too busy writing your ideal mate's attributes down, I'm out having fun and maybe finding the ideal mate or not...

While you are busy writing your vision board and putting pictures of 15 books that you want to emulate and the bookstores you want your books displayed at (on your pretty, laid-out cardboard), I'm typing away and having fun, not worrying about a vision board...

While you may be "pumping" yourself up with goals of losing 20 pounds in 2013...

The person who just lives a healthy lifestyle is just...living a healthy lifestyle. Oh yeah, the healthy person was doing that in 2012 too, while you were writing your goals for last year.

I invite you to try something new this year.

What would happen if you didn't give importance to your goals, but instead said to yourself:

"I will do the best I can do this year and every year, and whatever result comes from living freely is the exact result that is going to happen, whether I set goals or not."

What if instead of spending hours, months, or years writing down what your ideal mate is, you said to yourself:

"I am going to serve, love and trust myself and my instincts. I may be wrong with some of my instincts, but the beautiful part is, I may be right. The journey itself is part of the beauty, as well as the pleasures and pains in between. I will do the best this year and every year, and whatever result comes from living freely is the exact result that was going to happen, whether I set goals or not!"

When you remove yourself from focusing on your goals, you open yourself up to do what you wanted to do anyway...whether you made a vision board, dartboard, or a goal-setting whatcha-ma-call-it, or not.

It's time to go do what you want to do, not because you "goaled" yourself to do it, but because it's what you desire. You'll be surprised by how your mind and body will love you for it, just because you are being...YOU!

Have a wonderful New Year (for any year that is coming up) and live your life like you want!

**You can read more about the failure of goal setting at:

http://www.psychologytoday.com/blog/wired-success/201104/why-goal-setting-doesnt-work

It is a man's own mind, not his enemy or foe, which lures him to evil ways.

~Buddha

MEET YOUR THERAPIST
FREDDY KRUEGER

You may already know the story behind Freddy Krueger from *A Nightmare on Elm Street*.

He was a disfigured serial killer who used a glove armed with razors to kill his victims in their dreams, causing their death in the waking world, as well. However, when you take Freddy from "Dream World" into the "Real World," he has normal human vulnerability.

Freddy's trademarked burned, disfigured face, red and dark-green-striped sweater, brown fedora and the metal-clawed brown leather glove on his right hand, are things that kept me up all night...under the covers, scared to go to sleep and dream.

Freddy Krueger would probably be a better therapist, coach, and counselor than most in the mental wellness industry. Many in the wellness industry have good intentions, but are missing the key ingredients to living a stable, happy life.

If you followed Freddy Krueger and listened to what he taught us, 99.9 percent of so-called issues we suffer from would be resolved...INSTANTLY!

You see, Freddy Krueger has no real power, unless you fall asleep. The deeper you fall asleep, the stronger he becomes in your dreams. As soon as you wake up, what happens?

HE DISAPPEARS!

As soon as you wake up, he has no power; he can't harm you and no longer exists.

Let's try this again.

If you fall asleep, he comes to life and he can harm you. When you realize that you are in a dream, acknowledge that you're dreaming; become aware of it, and wake your ass up!

THAT'S IT!

As soon as you wake up, he completely vanishes. He can't hurt you anymore.

Here is the deal. If you don't wake up, whatever he does in the dream becomes real!

In other words, if he decides to slice and dice you in your dream, you are sliced and diced in real life!

If you are lucky, he'll do it quickly!

Okay — I think you get it.

You are probably wondering what Freddy has to do with your well-being, and you may even expect me to wrap this story up with a pretty ribbon on it.

The reality is, there is no pretty ribbon to wrap around

it at all. The connection is so real, people are killing themselves because of it. The truth is so scary that people are destroying perfectly good relationships with their loved ones. The story of Freddy Krueger and the metaphor to our lives is so real that people who are stressed out are getting ulcers, sleep apnea, paranoia, insomnia, anorexia, bulimia, and yes, even taking their own lives.

We all have a Freddy Krueger in our lives. We all have a way to remove Freddy Krueger out of our reality so he can't harm us. The problem is: we get so deep into this dream called *thought* that it becomes too late. It consumes us like a nightmare, and we think we don't have control anymore.

Freddy Krueger is not real!

Your thoughts are not real!

Let me rephrase that...

Your thoughts don't have power until you allow them the power!

When you wake up knowing that Freddy is just a dream, he can't hurt you.

When you realize that you are just harboring a thought, allowing it to brew in your mind, even though it doesn't carry any weight, energy or power...you just made it real.

The sick truth is...

Your thoughts are FREDDY KRUEGER, and you are the person who can choose to give it power, or let it pass, like all the other thoughts in your mind that you simply don't give two shits about.

That's the reality of it.

In a study at UCLA, they estimated that we have 70,000 thoughts a day!

Seventy-thousand thoughts.

In other words, you and I are really no different. We have the exact same amount of thoughts.

I have just realized that giving thought number 65,432 no more importance than thought 22,987 has given me a peace of mind that I couldn't find from a self-help book, or so-called professional who tells me to keep talking about my thoughts; reliving a particular event, every time.

I know that if I was stuck in my thinking, I could remind myself that this is just one thought out of 70,000 thoughts in a day. By making myself aware of this, that particular thought loses power.

Awareness of thought = SOLUTION!

We've been taught that we need to think about things; that we need to "work" on our thoughts.

This is like saying, "Keep dreaming about Freddy Krueger so he doesn't come after us." The problem is, Freddy only shows up in our dreams. The only way you'll remove him from your life is by realizing that "it's only a dream!" There is absolutely nothing else you need to do!

Your thoughts work this same way...

If you stay in your negative thought, you will kill yourself: emotionally, mentally or physically.

PERIOD!

So, what do you do when you are stuck in a thought like, *I just lost a loved one.*

I'd like to preface this with saying that I do not take death lightly.

I know many of my readers have lost a loved one.
I have also lost loved ones.

If you are like me, you probably recognize that while sitting in your thought about the loss of this loved one, you are hurting the most.

So what do we try to do?

We try to forget our thoughts as if they will go away.
It seems like the best way we know of to cope with the feeling.

We'll go play sports, watch a movie, talk to friends, go to yoga, or do anything we can to get out of our thoughts.

The reality is, it's just a temporary fix and we know it.

We know that you can try to forget thoughts, but thoughts are "thoughting" all day with or without your permission.

As we know from studies previously mentioned, we will have approximately 70,000 thoughts. Many of those thoughts, if not all of them, have no rhyme or reason…they just pop up in your head.

So, what can you do?

What if you don't have to keep yourself occupied?

What can you do with all the thoughts that come in?

What if you look at these thoughts for what they are — at face value?

What would happen?

You would know that thought is merely a speck of immaterial images that needs to be plugged into your consciousness before it can bear any meaning.

Thoughts need YOU to give them substance.

Thoughts need YOU to make the immaterial real,

before it becomes an ulcer, depression, anger, or sadness.

Thoughts need YOU to make them real; like dreams need Freddy to become real.
When the dreamer realizes it's just a dream...Freddy disappears.

When the person having a thought realizes it's just another thought, the sadness, anger, and grief begin to disappear.

I get suckered by my thoughts, too.

I don't want anyone to think that I am any different.

My life has become easier since discovering my mental distress is created by my own thoughts.

Have you ever had a fight with your girlfriend, husband, etc., and everyone else seems to know the kind of advice to give you?

At the time, you just don't see it the way everyone else does.

Why?

It's because you are pre-occupied with your own thoughts.

You are trying to get rid of Freddy, while you're still

dreaming.

If your friend was going through the exact same thing, you would be able to give them sound advice.

Do you know why?

You are not in their thinking!

That's why people say, "I don't know why I can give others great advice, but I can't give myself the same advice!"

It's the same reason that the server in the movie was able to wake up the guy in the restaurant before Freddy got him. The server was awake, but the guy fell asleep.

Others seem to come up with answers to our problems because...

They aren't putting as much THOUGHT into your problem.

That's why they can help you.

We've been suckered to think that by giving two shits about our THOUGHTS, we are going to come to a better resolution.

We think that by giving miserable thought MORE THINKING, we are going to come to a better answer.

I know the opposite to be true.

I have had people argue with me by saying I'm making it too easy.

But what if the answer was just that easy?

I'm human. I know what you're going through because I've had pain, anger, sadness, and guilty thoughts.

I've decided that by being a bystander of my thoughts, life is easier. I let thoughts go…like a passerby looking at cars. I don't give one car more meaning than the next when they're zipping by.

When I become a bystander of ALL my thoughts, they don't have the same meaning they once had.

As soon as I get stuck in a thought, I remind myself… it's just another thought.

Like I said, I don't take depression, PTSD, or any mental struggle lightly. And I know for damn sure that those events are very painful to deal with.

Hear me out.

Depression and anger go through the exact same mechanism that thinking about your dinner does. We just think that by giving the thought about grieving more meaning, it will resolve something.

Most of the time, it doesn't.

The reality is, when I talk to my clients, some will fight me tooth and nail about this concept.

I also know for many of my clients, it just clicks one day and they'll say…"Shit, you're right! Why did I spend so much time doing that! Why did I spend so much time thinking and thinking about it? Thinking wasn't the problem. Giving the thinking power was the problem!"

Matter of fact, I don't agree with therapists who tell you to relive a trauma.

If I am correct with my assumption, more thinking about the situation is not the answer.

If you have been traumatized by rape, Post-Traumatic Stress Disorder, or something terrible from the past… who came up with the idea to bring it up again to find a resolution?

If someone has been raped once, why the hell do they have to go through it again?

Personally, I think one time is enough. I'd rather show them how thoughts work, so they can go back to living a peaceful life.

I don't think that therapists are making their clients relive the past to harm them. I think that for many of them, it's the only way they know how to help them.

It's what they have been taught. It's what studies have shown. Studies are good, if you are studying the right subject.

Imagine if the therapists were doing a study about "Which stick would hurt less if you were to get hit with one."

A stick made of bark or bamboo?
A study would probably say you should get hit with a bark stick and they could prove why this is the best choice, study after study.

I would like the client to know that they don't have to be hit by either stick...they can walk away.

That would solve the issue.

Instead, many people are still getting hit with sticks because studies, books, and therapists have told them which option (of two) would be less painful...

Showing people that all feelings and emotions (by default) travel through our thoughts, and dealing with thoughts directly becomes a better alternative.

No matter how you look at it, everyone's feelings and thoughts need a home in order to survive. It's only by bringing thoughts into our consciousness that they come alive.

So, telling someone to relive a trauma every time they sit in a therapist's office is counterproductive. You are spending the client's time in the wrong place.

You are keeping the client in their thoughts in an attempt to have them remove their thinking.

That's like telling someone to remove Freddy Krueger from their life by going back into the dream. The problem is in the dream!

<u>The way to get out of the dream is to just be aware that it's a dream.</u>

THE WAY TO GET OUT OF YOUR NEGATIVE THOUGHTS IS TO REALIZE THAT THEY'RE NOT NEGATIVE OR POSITIVE...IT'S JUST ONE THOUGHT OUT OF 70,000 THAT COMES ALIVE, IF YOU CHOOSE TO PLUG INTO ANY ONE THOUGHT.

I want to offer you an invitation.

I want to invite you to a **Paradigm Shift**.

I am inviting you to not grasp on to a thought that's making you feel terrible.

For many who have dealt with a traumatic past...the good news is, it's in the past.

For many who have worries for the future...the beautiful part is...it's not here yet, so you can let those thoughts pass through freely.

The only way to relive trauma is to soak yourself in those traumatic feelings, bringing them back up into the vicious circle of thought.

That's really the only way. There is no other way it holds power!

This is the new paradigm to balancing the weight these problems, issues, and dilemmas actually hold.

It may even be counterintuitive to what you may have been taught.

I invite you to try it.

When you have a thought, tell yourself it's just a thought.
Invite yourself to step back and let that thought go by.

If it decides to stay for a bit, let it. The reality is, you don't have much of a choice anyway.

Have you really had any choice when a thought is going to arise or stay? Tell me about your first thought upon waking up...what permitted that thought to enter?

Once you've let go of controlling your thoughts, allowing them to play in your headspace where they really have no power, see what happens.

You'll soon realize that you don't need to go anywhere to calm yourself down. You'll realize that it's not yoga class, or the beach, or anywhere else that gives you peace of mind. You'll realize that you gave your thoughts less importance and that's why you feel better.

Each of us has the power to become aware of this skill. It's not the outside environment that will bring you to mental well-being, it's the inside awareness that takes you there.

I know this may seem too easy.
But what if it is?

Be mindful that you're not brushing this idea that I propose away, simply because it seems too easy...

Do you know what's happened to the mental health industry because they've tried finding answers from everywhere else?

They continue creating branches of psychotherapy in search of answers.

There are an estimated 400 different types of therapy hoping to solve this mental crisis. Many of the therapies are just a better stick to get hit with, rather than a solution.

We're looking for answers from the thousands of books on self-help that tell you what you should do, while they all contradict and fight each other.

If someone came to me and asked me what they

should do about the pain of a break-up, I know that the answer is simple. I would say the same thing I would say to the person who is dreaming about Freddy Krueger. Realize it's a dream and he goes away...

Realize your pain doesn't exist somewhere "out there" — it's just a thought. Realize that you're giving that ONE thought MORE meaning than any of the other thoughts that are going through your head. Each thought has the same amount of weight as the one you are stuck on. Become aware that it's just a speck among the 70,000 other thoughts that will flow through today.

When you truly get this understanding, the thought just goes away (or doesn't have the power you gave it). The thoughts really have no choice but to disappear, because you decided you don't want to play with that thought anymore.

Once you go back to seeing a thought for what it is... it's easy to get back to your life.

The thoughts don't have strength to be hurtful.

There won't be a Freddy Krueger to worry about.

You'll know that he can only be hurtful when you stay in your dream of thoughts...

Truth is not something outside to be discovered, it is something inside to be realized.

~**Osho**

IF I HAD A DIARY ENTRY THIS WOULD BE IN IT...

It's not about being happy. The idea is not to find a way to be happy. No, not at all. The problem of trying to find happiness assumes our default is that we don't have it.

Doing nothing is an understanding.

It's when you look farther to see what's behind all emotions. It's a realization that happiness, sadness, anger, or any emotion does not or cannot exist unless it's thought about.

In other words, happiness is not a thing, or a part of who we are.

Happiness is just a word, a construct to make sense of our world.

There is no such thing as happiness in the "outside" sense of the world. In other words, you cannot obtain happiness from material goods. You can think that material goods make you happy. A vacation does not bring you happiness. It may settle your thoughts just enough for you to feel inner peace, which in turn can make you feel happy.

We sometimes connect happiness as something

that we need to grab, obtain and hold on to. Good luck. It's been tried and it has failed!

But why do we keep doing it?

Because the answer is so easy we miss it!

It's kind of a game of hide and seek. You've seen it before!

My dad, time and time again, would search for his eyeglasses all over the house! We would look at him and laugh...just enough for him to realize they'd been on his head the whole time.

Happiness works the same way! It's a part of us, just like sadness is a part of us. But not in a way that you see it. It's a part of our thoughts that travel in our heads. It has no real power; it zips through our consciousness, gliding at a ghostly speed. We have to STOP IT, grab a hold of it, and say YES! I want to feel this way.

Otherwise, if you see it like a wave in the ocean, it will pass. And when it passes, in comes a new thought.

Like the five o'clock train, if you miss it, don't you worry, thousands more will come! The interesting thing about our thoughts is, they do their "thoughting" without you. They don't really need your input. It won't matter if you give any input.

Actually, it will matter only in the fact that you will reduce your innate wisdom by adding your input.

By adding your input, your two cents, you constrict new thoughts from arising.

Don't give power to any thought, and you'll be able to receive its gift to make better decisions, clearer outcomes, and inner peace and wisdom.

You have an endless supply of powerful thoughts to aid you, guide you, and keep you on your toes!

But be careful! As soon as you think thoughts are worth more than what they are, they disappear and mold into the very thing you may not want them to become — anger, frustration, etc.

The cool thing is, once you become the bystander of your thoughts, you can pluck any thought out you want and play with it and give it meaning. That's when we blossom with "aha" moments, insights! That's when you realize that your glasses have been on you all along and you realize that your vision is 20/20!

So, if giving power to bad thoughts makes them real, then why isn't it true for good thoughts?

It is!

Have you had a fantasy that you made real? Did you feel it in your body? Did it give you a tingly feeling? Can you feel it now?

It seems that for our happy thoughts, we know that they are just thoughts for the most part. It's the bad ones that we bring to life for a longer period of time. It's the bad ones that we think that if we hold on to them longer, they will resolve our predicament.

Those are the thoughts we need to watch out for. Those are the thoughts that we think have power. They don't!

YOU GIVE THEM POWER!

As soon as you know it's just one thought plucked out of the thousands you're going to have, the thought goes back to the river of thoughts and your body settles, finds peace!

I remember having a speaking phobia. I would pace around the room, thinking about what I would say on stage, lose my appetite, and do all sorts of rituals to help myself remove this fear.

Great!

I was trying to do more thinking to stop myself from thinking! The funny thing is, this was months before I spoke!

How was this a real phobia? It wasn't...I would have dreadful thoughts of speaking, so I'd decide to pluck those thoughts and mold them into my reality. All of a sudden my body would feel it. I would give the sensations more thinking. Then I would think more about the sensations, about the stage fright, which got me thinking about whether I should even do the damn talk! Wow, all of this from the streams of thought in my head!

One day, I decided to step back and become aware that it's just a thought.

Just a fucking thought in my head!!!

All of it!

Just a thought!

Something very interesting happened...

I couldn't get myself to be scared anymore. I don't know what happened.

I wanted to test this out again, but the problem was...it was too late!

My body and brain and thinking already knew that I was just one thought away from not worrying about it, so I stopped worrying. It (my head) realized that I didn't care anymore, so it decided to let other thoughts through...

Does that mean I don't think about being scared on stage? Of course, my brain still does it. But it's so nice to know that it means as much as the thinking telling me whether I should go pee, or take out the trash! All thoughts are made from the same fabric! One doesn't hold more meaning than the other.

That's just it!

Now when I get on stage, as soon as a thought about preparation comes to mind, or being scared, I smile and move on. Sometimes I play a game with myself and say, "Cool, Amir, that's an interesting thought..." and I just move on!

What a freedom I have received! I had tried everything before. I had tried Hypnosis, NLP, positive psychology, I read books, went to seminars, and did everything to remove my fear...

The only thing I didn't do was try NOTHING!

Now I get on stage and I don't think about anything until I am on stage. I can grab a bite to eat, take a nap, read a book...whatever.

The thoughts are in the background as they always are. They just don't have the effect they once had.

I mean, think about it — we don't give it much thought when we change the TV channel, so why do we think that if we give speaking more thought it will do anything for us? Speaking in front of 200 people is no different to me now than changing the channel on a TV.

Others may think that one has more meaning than the other. But I know it's just their thinking about one event vs. the other.

Think about it — why aren't you scared for me when I speak? It's because you couldn't care less whether I'm on stage or not. So why the hell do I think that if I think more about it than you, it's better or worse for me? I might as well put as much thought into it as you, right?

So, at this point people say, "So, are you saying just don't care?"

No, I am saying give relevance to the *event*, but not the *thinking* about the event. When you give relevance to *thinking* about the event, you cannot see the event for what it is because your thinking clouds what is actually happening (the event).

I care passionately about what I do. The problem was, my thinking was getting in the way of being able to communicate my message! I had a full-time job working overtime in my thoughts! One job was trying to remove or reduce the thinking in my head. The other was figuring out my talks and planning for them.

I got rid of one of my jobs and now I can strictly focus on what's important...going on stage and speaking to my audience.

Just knowing and understanding this little piece of wisdom will help you in every aspect of your life.

Trust me!

Imagine if you stopped allowing your thinking to get between you and your love life.

What about all of the thinking that made you lose sleep over your job?

What about the thinking about traffic that you were so pre-occupied with...it's just another thought out of the thousands you will have that day...can you see that if you don't give it relevance, how much freedom you can have?

The only shackles we have are the shackles of thoughts. The thoughts we think are more than merely our neurology flashing signs in our brain, as if they are real. They aren't!

Become a bystander and enjoy the neurological light show, flashing thoughts at light speed! Laugh at the silly ones, oohh and aaahh at the ones that look scary. It's funny, interesting, and...it's just a thought!

So, what do you have to do, you may ask?

All you have to do is do NOTHING! From the awareness of letting thoughts stream in your mind, you see them for what they are, wordless, scentless flow of "thought essence" moving around your head. Just watch them, don't do anything more.

From this nothing, all sorts of moments spring up. The increments of enlightenment, the aha moments, and everything in-between.

It's all nothing. Now isn't that something?

stillpower n. The clarity of mind to live with freedom and ease; the inner source of excellence; the opposite of willpower.

~Garret Kramer

Question: Why do we store up flattery and insult, hurt and affection?

Why do we store up flattery and insult, hurt and affection? Without this accumulation of experiences and their responses, we are not; we are nothing if we have no name, no attachment, no belief. It is the fear of being nothing that compels us to accumulate; and it is this very fear, whether conscious or unconscious, that, in spite of our accumulative activities, brings about our disintegration and destruction. If we can be aware of the truth of this fear, then it is the truth that liberates us from it, and not our purposeful determination to be free, You are nothing. You may have your name and title, your property and bank account, you may have power and be famous; but in spite of all these safeguards, you are as nothing. You may be totally unaware of this emptiness, this nothingness, or you may simply not want to be aware of it; but it is there, do what you will to avoid it. You may try to escape from it in devious ways, through personal or collective violence, through individual or collective worship, through knowledge or amusement; but whether you are asleep or awake, it is always there. You can come upon your relationship to this nothingness and its fear only by being choicelessly aware of the escapes. You are not related to it as a separate, individual entity; you are not the observer watching it; without you, the thinker, the observer, it is not. You and nothingness are one; you and nothingness are a joint phenomenon, not two separate processes. If you, the thinker, are afraid of it and approach it as something contrary and opposed to you, then any action you may take towards it must inevitably lead to illusion and so to further conflict and misery. When there is the discovery, the experiencing of that nothingness as you, then fear - which exists only when the thinker is separate from his thoughts and so tries to establish a relationship with them - completely drops away. Only then is it possible for the mind to be still; and in this tranquility, truth comes into being.

(Commentaries on Living Series I Self-Defence—
J. Krishnamurti)

We shape clay into a pot, but it is the emptiness inside that holds whatever we want.

~ Zen Saying

FOR THE SCIENTIST:
BY NOW EVERYTHING I HAVE BEEN SAYING MAY BE CONFUSING FOR THE SCIENCE MINDED.
IF THAT IS THE CASE... I HAVE A TREAT FOR YOU.
THE SCIENTIFIC EXPLANATION FOR THIS TYPE OF THINKING:

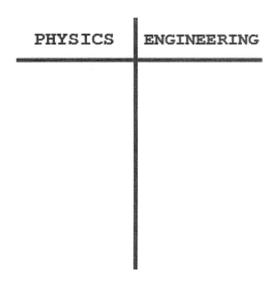

Take a look at the T-Bar Diagram above. I want you to imagine that we want to build an airplane. On the right, I will put the engineering that may take place, on the left the physics behind the engineering.

If we put some of the engineering on the right, we would need some things like CAD drawings, graphs, physical parts of the plane, etc. (Keep in mind I am not an engineer. Bear with me and understand the idea behind the idea!)

PHYSICS	ENGINEERING
	*CAD Drawings
	*Graphs
	*Physical parts of the plane
	*Computer Animation tools
	*Design Plans
	*Landing Gear

*The idea behind the engineering is that the engineering is the physical stuff needed to build the plane. By physical I mean even abstract things like numbers that can be translated into physical things like the length of a wing size, or the tires, etc.

The physics behind building the airplane are things like the laws of gravity, laws of motion, centrifugal force, etc.

PHYSICS	ENGINEERING
*Laws of Gravity *Laws of Motion *Laws of Force *Laws of Pressure Etc.	*CAD Drawings *Graphs *Physical parts of the plane *Computer Animation tools *Design Plans *Landing Gear

*The physics is the understanding behind the engineering. It's the laws that govern the engineering.

I know you're probably wondering what this has to do with inner peace and well-being. I promise I'll get to that!

The idea behind the simplified drawing is that the engineering is only as good as the understanding we have behind the laws that govern the engineering.

If an engineer couldn't figure out why the wing he designed is not allowing the plane to go up, he would need to see if the engineering fits with the laws of gravity, motion, etc.

Can we agree that the engineer who has a better understanding of how the laws work will have better engineering? If he didn't have a clue about the laws of gravity and how they worked, would it really matter what program he was using or the style of the wing?

The engineer would be banging his head wondering why the plane is not flying!

Another engineer who understood the laws of gravity would easily see that the wing the other engineer was making is not going to work, just by understanding the laws.

The other engineer could frustrate himself by changing the color of the wing, adding stars to the wing, putting glitter on the wing or what have you, but if he doesn't know how the physics work behind the engineering, the engineering is practically worthless. Transversely, the greater his understanding of the physics of a particular subject, the better the engineering will be.

The same idea applies to our thinking!

Most of us try to fix an emotional problem by changing the engineering. We think if we do things like change our thinking, do positive affirmations, read more about why we are like this, buy a car, try to forget our thoughts, yoga, go on vacation, change relationships or our environment, etc., it will bring us closer to inner peace.

PHYSICS	ENGINEERING
	*Positive Affirmations
	*Buying a Car
	*New Relationships
	*Read More
	*Forget your thoughts
	*Vacation
	*Think Happy Thoughts
	*Alternative Approaches

Now, I don't want you to think that doing any of the stuff mentioned above does not work or won't make you feel better. All I am saying is, once you know the physics behind all the "things" we can do to find inner peace, you may very well see that it's not necessary or even beneficial to do any of those to find inner peace or wisdom. After you understand the physics behind the way our inner peace works, you can use or do any of the "engineering" as you please, but you won't rely on them anymore to bring you inner peace. You'll know that trying to fix the "engineering" will become irrelevant for the task. That is a great relief!

With that being said, the physics behind all the engineering is very simple. If by now you've read the other parts of the book, you should be able to answer the question...what is the physics behind all the engineering that we believe brings us inner peace?

Everything on the right-hand side that we feel gives us clarity is simply one thing and one thing alone: the understanding that when our mind is calm, we can do anything better. What do I mean by "calm"?

When we understand that anything we do is first filtered by a thought and a thought is given power solely by the person who is observing it, we can find inner peace anywhere, at any time! This is not a knowledge-based system, this is just an understanding that as soon as you "get it," it instantly calms you; it instantly allows you to see things that you may not have seen before.

The interesting thing about the physics behind the system to well-being is that our thoughts pass through our heads by the second, and we have the choice to choose which thoughts we want to play with. Sometimes a thought like, "Should I do the dishes?" will pass through your head. You then make the decision to make it important or not.

If the thought that you may get fired comes into your mind, you may think that's more important than doing the dishes. The truth of the matter is, in reality they are just thoughts in your head. If you treat it as such, and not make one more important than another, your body's natural mechanism will give you the insights and wisdom you need to make clear decisions about what you may or may not need to do in the situation regarding your job.

The cosmic mistake we make is that we think if we get absorbed by our thinking and allow one particular thought, like losing our job, to have more importance than another thought, we are going to get some sort of insight. We are actually constricting wisdom's ability to come through. It's like trying to unclog the kitchen drain by putting more food in it. Putting more thinking into thinking just brings you more thinking!

Understanding that it's just a thought and wasting your time engaging in that one thought is just a futile attempt at nothing. Matter of fact, it's counterproductive to get the insights you need to resolve the issue.

This may appear like another thing to do, but it's not. This is NOT another engineering idea to put in place of another one.

Matter of fact, in order to do this, there is nothing to do. There is no system, tool, or idea to put in place. It's something that we do most of the time when we have inner peace. We just think we need to do something else when we see something troubling. But if we follow the understanding that a thought is just a thought, that is the extent of all you need to know to get your insights, aha moments, and inner peace.

That is the physics behind everything! It's that a thought is just a thought. There is NOTHING you need to do. Just see things for what they are, nothing more, nothing less...

PHYSICS	ENGINEERING
Inner peace can only be created with our awareness of our THOUGHTS! The less thinking, the more peace we have.	*Positive Affirmations *Buying a Car *New Relationships *Read More *Forget your thoughts *Vacation *Think Happy Thoughts *Alternative Approaches

We can do all the engineering we want to create inner peace. Once we understand the concept of giving one thought no more or less significance than another thought, our body and thinking naturally resorts to less effort and more insights and inner peace.

Your assignment is to stop putting so much emphasis on the engineering to obtain inner peace and become aware of the system behind the system.

All you need to know is anger, sadness, hurt, and frustration are just a thought away to remove them. In other words, they're not sitting anywhere but in your thoughts. You don't need to do anything. You don't need to try to stop it, fake it,

remove it or replace it. All you need to do is understand...it's just another thought your mind is having out of thousands more it will have.

I know you want to do something about it...

It's time to do NOTHING ABOUT IT!

It is the thought-life that pollutes.
~Jesus Christ

Life repeats itself mindlessly – unless you become mindful, it will go on repeating like a wheel. That's why Buddhists call it the wheel of life and death – the wheel of time. It moves like a wheel: birth followed by death, death is followed by birth: love is followed by hate, hate is followed by love; success followed by failure, failure followed by success. Just see!

If you can watch just for a few days, you will see a pattern emerging, a wheel pattern. One day, a fine morning, you are feeling so good and so happy, and another day you are so dull, so dead that you can start thinking of committing suicide. And just the other day you were so full of life, so blissful that you were feeling thankful to God that you were in a mood of deep gratefulness, and today there is great complaint and you don't see the point of why one should go on living...And it goes on and on, but you don't see the pattern.

Once you see the pattern, you can get out of it.

Take it Easy, Vol. 1, Chapter 7 by Osho

Just One Thought...

You are just ONE thought away from happiness.

You are just ONE thought away from sadness.

You are just ONE thought away from joy.

You are just ONE thought away from inner peace.

You are just ONE thought away from stopping the noise.

You are just ONE thought away from guilt.

You are just ONE thought away from suicidal thinking.

You are just ONE thought away from depression.

You are just ONE thought away from giving up.

You are just ONE thought away from hurting yourself.

You are Just ONE thought away from another thought.

You are Just **One thought** away from Perfect Health*

*IT'S JUST A THOUGHT. THAT'S IT! YOU DON'T HAVE TO DO ANY MORE THAN KNOW IT'S JUST A THOUGHT. ONE THOUGHT HAS NO MORE POWER THAN ANOTHER. WE MAKE BELIEVE THAT ONE IS WORTH MORE THAN ANOTHER. WE ARE FREE TO CHOOSE THE ONE WE WANT TO GIVE POWER TO. WHY GIVE POWER TO THE ONE THAT HURTS US? IT'S LIKE THE BIG BAD BOOGEY MAN. AS SOON AS WE KNOW HE DOESN'T REALLY EXIST…HE DISAPPEARS.

EXCERPT FROM THE FILM *REVOLVER* ABOUT THOUGHTS:

You heard the voice for so long you believe it to be you.

You believe it to be your best friend.

You believe your opponent to be your best friend.

Where's the best place your opponent should hide?

The very last place you would ever look…

Do you know who Sam Gold (your thoughts) is, Mister Green?

You should…because he knows who you are.

The Gold…Sam Gold…Mr. Clandestine…Mr. Ambiguous…Mr. Mystery…

It's all up here (pointing to his head)…**Pretending to be you!**

THOUGHT **THOUGHT** THOUGHT **THOUGHT** THOUGHT THOUGHT THOUGHT **THOUGHT** THOUGHT THOUGHT THOUGHT **THOUGHT** THOUGHT THOUGHT THOUGHT THOUGHT THOUGHT **THOUGHT** THOUGHT THOUGHT THOUGHT THOUGHT THOUGHT THOUGHT **THOUGHT** **THOUGHT** THOUGHT THOUGHT THOUGHT THOUGHT THOUGHT THOUGHT THOUGHT **THOUGHT** THOUGHT THOUGHT **THOUGHT** THOUGHT THOUGHT THOUGHT **THOUGHT** THOUGHT THOUGHT THOUGHT THOUGHT THOUGHT THOUGHT THOUGHT THOUGHT THOUGHT THOUGHT THOUGHT THOUGHT THOUGHT **THOUGHT** THOUGHT THOUGHT THOUGHT **THOUGHT** THOUGHT **THOUGHT** THOUGHT THOUGHT THOUGHT THOUGHT THOUGHT THOUGHT THOUGHT THOUGHT **THOUGHT** THOUGHT THOUGHT THOUGHT THOUGHT THOUGHT THOUGHT THOUGHT **THOUGHT** THOUGHT **THOUGHT** THOUGHT THOUGHT THOUGHT THOUGHT THOUGHT **THOUGHT** THOUGHT **THOUGHT** THOUGHT **THOUGHT** THOUGHT THOUGHT

The person with true innate well-being knows that thoughts don't have any rhyme or reason. Someone with true well-being understands that thoughts all look like what you see above. Just a string of nothingness. I decided to **bold** the thoughts I wanted. You can do that too (in your mind). That's what free will offers. But don't worry about one thought more than another. Thoughts are so fleeting. No point in holding on to any particular one. Unless you want to. It's your choice...

ATTENTION!

Turn the page for a shortcut to discover everything about this book!

(Everything on the next page is all you need to know!)

More About Nothing at:
www.amirkarkouti.com

DO NOTHING TO GET EVERYTHING
Copyright © by Amir Karkouti

All rights reserved. No part of this book may be reproduced or transmitted in any form or by any means, electronic or mechanical, including photocopying, recording or by any information storage and retrieval system, without written permission from the author, except for the inclusion of brief quotations in a review.

ISBN 13: 978-1-93974-500-2
ISBN 10: 1-93974-500-4
Library of Congress Control Number: 2013933728

Published by Old University Press